Garden Cuttings

Nina Alison Crone OAM
(21 August 1934 – 14 July 2007)

Garden Cuttings

ARTICLES FOR *THE AGE*
BY NINA CRONE

Edited by
HELEN FORGASZ

Australian Scholarly Publishing

First published 2008
Australian Scholarly Publishing Pty Ltd
7 Lt Lothian St Nth, North Melbourne, Vic 3051
Tel: 03 9329 6963 Fax: 03 9329 5452
Email: aspic@ozemail.com.au
Web: www.scholarly.info

A Cataloguing-in-Publication entry for this title is available
from the National Library of Australia.

ISBN 978 174 097 1928

Copyediting by Diane Carlyle
Design and typesetting by Mick Earls
Printing and binding by BPA Print Group

Proceeds from this book will be donated to Melbourne Girls
Grammar School. An academic prize for excellence in history, in
the name of Nina Alison Crone, will be established in perpetuity.

This book was published with the generous support of:

THE CRONE FAMILY

Melbourne Girls Grammar
an Anglican school

MONASH University
Education

AUSTRALIAN
**GARDEN
HISTORY**
SOCIETY

Contents

Foreword   xiii

Anne Latreille (former Editor of the Gardening section,
The Age)

Preface   xvii

Helen Forgasz

Acknowledgments   xx

Introduction   1

Helen Forgasz

SECTION 1:

Plants

Plants: introduction   17

Helen Forgasz

Setting a fashion for violets   19

(theme: violet, published: 11 March 1986)

The cabbage*   20

(cabbage, 15 April 1986)

Disraeli admired a humble flower   21

(primrose, 22 April 1986)

The heath*   22

(heath, 6 May 1986)

The flavour of mythology   23
(laurel, 27 May 1986)

A sour yet sweet favourite   25
(pomegranate, 17 June 1986)

The chrysanthemum*   26
(chrysanthemum, 1 July 1986)

Will Victoria's link with Venus prevail?   27
(myrtle, 22 July 1986)

Pineapples polled well as a gift   29
(pineapple, 12 August 1986)

A symbol of undying love   31
(winter gillyflower, 2 September 1986)

Thanks to Turks for the gift of tulips   32
(tulip, 30 September 1986)

The tree of Circe, the sorceress, still gives magic   35
(weeping willow, 28 October 1986)

River red gum: a tree for nostalgia   36
(red river gum, 16 December 1986)

Gentian and lobelia are the true-blues   38
(gentian and lobelia, 3 February 1987)

In love with a love apple   40
(tomato, 10 March 1987)

Adam's fall may be linked to his covering figleaves   42
(fig, 14 April 1987)

Ivy has a proud heritage   44
(ivy, 5 May 1987)

The Pasque flower*   45
(Pasque flower, 2 June 1987)

Pears have a rich heritage, by any name   46
(pear, 30 June 1987)

The harbinger of spring is good enough to eat   48
(lilac, 27 October 1987)

Language of flowers   50
(Christmas garland flowers, 22 December 1987)

The protea *   52
(protea, 23 February 1988)

A floral lesson of Christ's Passion   54
(passionfruit flower, 29 March 1988)

Touch of Mexican sun   55
(dahlia, 3 May 1988)

Symbol of love and fertility   57
(quince, 31 May 1988)

Sweet corn stands tall   58
(sweet corn, 21 June 1988)

Acacia Avenue, and no wattles in sight   60
(black locust or false acacia, 30 August 1988)

Sequoyah – the man and the tree   61
(sequoia, 13 December 1988)

Australia's beloved warrior   64
(waratah, 7 February 1989)

A lucky bouquet fit for a king   66
(lily-of-the-valley, 16 May 1989)

Birth of the red, white and blue   67
(Bastille Day flowers, 11 July 1989)

A shrub to refresh man's weariness   69
(camellia, 18 July 1989)

Spring brings magic of daffodil days   72
(daffodil, 19 September 1989)

Origin of the species is under a cloud   74
(fuchsia, 19 December 1989)

Aubergine – the Turks' gourmet delight   76
(aubergine, 5 June 1990)

Summer snow   78
(Australian Christmas plants, 23 December 1995)

Spinach   80
(spinach, unpublished)

Quandongs   82
(quandong, unpublished)

The iris   83
(iris, unpublished)

Geraniums and pelargoniums   85
(geranium and pelargonium, unpublished)

The Douglas Fir   88
(Douglas fir, unpublished)

Trees for the swagman and the smith   91
(coolabah and chestnut, unpublished)

*   Title provided by editor

SECTION 2:

Gardens

Gardens: introduction   93
Helen Botham

A world of contrasts waits in the Big Apple   95
(theme: Brooklyn Gardens, USA, published: 24 August 1984)

The occasional man fancies himself in paradise   98
(Hangzhou Gardens, China, 5 October 1984)

Italians savour a Scotsman's legacy   101
(Villa Taranto, Italy, 26 October 1984)

America's most civilised acres   104
(Dumbarton Oaks, USA, 30 November 1984)

Bagatelle it may be, but it is not mere rose garden   107
(Bagatelle, France, 28 December 1984)

Railroader's riches spawned a marvel of botany   110
(Huntington Gardens, USA, 8 February 1985)

Bogor, a venture in paradise   113
(Bogor Botanic Gardens, Indonesia, 8 March 1985)

San Fran fragrance on show   116
(Strybing Arboretum, USA, 4 April 1985)

Gardens in touch with the times   119
(National Botanic Gardens, Canberra, 3 May 1985)

Let the Brits take you up the garden path, historically   122
(Nymans, UK, 24 May 1985)

Edinburgh's plants were reared for their medicinal value   125
(Royal Botanic Gardens, Edinburgh, Scotland, 28 June 1985)

Cornwall's 'Farm of the spring' was built on
the proceeds of slavery   128
(Trengwainton, UK, 2 August 1985)

Behind many a great man is a great gardener   131
(Washington's USA and Cooks' Victoria gardens,
13 September 1985)

A garden's role in the flowering of peace
and understanding   134
(Cowra Peace Garden, NSW, 16 September 1986)

Fashion of the Tudors finds modern flavour   137
(Knot gardens, 16 June 1987)

Heatwave evokes memories of Athens' cooler corners   140
(Athens, Greece, 4 August 1987)

Gardens in Leningrad, USSR 142
(Leningrad, former USSR, unpublished)

Tashkent, Uzbekistan, USSR 146
(Tashkent, former USSR, unpublished)

Moorish gardens in Spain 149
(gardens in Spain, unpublished)

Royal Botanic Gardens, Hobart 152
(Hobart Botanic Gardens, unpublished)

Darling Harbour's Friendship Garden 155
(Chinese Garden, Darling Harbour, Sydney, unpublished)

SECTION 3:

Close to Home

Close to home: introduction 159
Helen Forgasz

MELBOURNE

Following the tree trail 161
(theme: American trees, Royal Botanic Gardens, Melbourne,
published: 8 October 1982)

A question of identity 164
(Royal Botanic Gardens, Melbourne, 25 November 1986)

Nature flourishes amid the city's heavy traffic 165
(Melbourne's iconic trees, 15 October 1985)

Exploring our squares is rewarding 167
(Melbourne's squares, 7 January 1986)

Delight and inspiration at Garden Week 1986   170
(Garden Week 1986, 18 March 1986)

Measuring success by the departing plants   172
(Garden Week 1987, 17 March 1987)

Themes of visual delight   174
(Garden Week 1988, 22 March 1988)

Garden Week has grand designs   176
(Garden Week 1989, 21 March 1989)

GIPPSLAND

Venus by the sea   178
(Kitchen garden, Venus Bay, 28 October 1995)

Morwell's communal celebration in roses   181
(Morwell rose garden, 25 November 1995)

The Strzelecki serenades   183
(Music festival, Mossvale, Gippsland, 24 February 1996)

Making plans   185
(Using a garden designer, Nina's Walkerville property,
16 March 1996)

Garden success stories: Nina Crone – retired school principal   189
(Nina's Walkerville garden, 5 April 1997)

EDUCATIONAL MISCELLANY

Careers in horticulture (Part 1)   190
(4 January 1985)

Look at becoming a career horticulturist (Part 2)   194
(11 January 1985)

The Art of Nature Printing   200
(Nature printing, Coolart, Somers, Victoria, 10 December 1985)

Endangered species list grows   202
(honey-myrtle on World Wildlife Fund endangered
plants list, 11 February 1986)

A resourceful way to learn about trees   205
(trees and forest kit, 14 October 1986)

Indulge with simplicity   207
(spring – arranging cut flowers, 25 November 1986)

Plots of the rich and famous   210
(book review: *The Rothschild Gardens*, 12 April 1997)

Foreword

ANNE LATREILLE
former Editor of the Gardening section of *The Age*

Lively, energetic, erudite. This was the Nina Crone I knew.
She was a born teacher, constantly seeking to expand and
pass on her knowledge. She loved language, plants fascinated
her, and she really enjoyed gardening. All of which made her an
ideal contributor to the Gardening section of *The Age*.

I inherited Nina as a contributor when I took over this
section in 1985. She was immediately helpful and encouraging to
her new editor, who knew less about gardens and gardening
than she did. At first I wasn't aware of her true identity, because
somewhat mysteriously, she chose to write under a pseudonym,
but this simply added a slight *frisson* to our initial dealings. And
it didn't matter, as her work was of uniformly high quality.

My goals for the Gardening section were ambitious.
Continuing the work of Tommy Garnett, my revered predecessor,
I wanted to build up a readership that put gardening in a
broader context than one's own backyard. With the aim of
encouraging gardeners who really thought about what they were
doing, I sought to publish articles that promoted not only the
time-honoured practical aspects of gardening, but also its
aesthetic, philosophical and historic aspects, and most important
of all, its place in relation to the Australian landscape and
environment.

Nina understood perfectly and, fitting her writing into an
action-packed life, proved to be a willing, enthusiastic and
prolific helper. She contributed the quirky 'Plants in History'
column, as well as occasional articles drawn from wherever she
happened to find herself, be it country New South Wales or the
heart of Paris.

Here are extracts from a letter written in February 1989. She had been in her beloved France with a group of students from Melbourne Girls Grammar, where she was headmistress. The letter was accompanied by a sheaf of articles, for my possible use throughout the coming year. It exudes the joy of experience in another part of the world, and her delight in history. It shows her forward-looking attitude and her awareness of others – for she greatly enjoyed people, as well as plants!

Dear Anne,

A rather mixed assortment herewith enclosed. They [the articles] *were started at various times last year – usually when the subject was in flower or fruit. I guess they will keep until next season and give you the opportunity, if you wish, of suggesting companion pieces of a more horticultural nature.*

My host family in Angoulême was quite charming – a wonderful house originally owned by Utrillo and on the banks of the Charente. It was not the season for the garden although imagination could picture it in the full beauty of summer roses. Monsieur was a keen amateur gardener and we dined often on his home-grown poireaux [leeks] …

… Paris was a rush – impossible in 2 and a half days – the city was embarking on the bicentennial celebrations of the Revolution and I caught the tail-end of some exhibitions commemorating the bicentenary of Buffon's birth/death (1788).

At the bookshop in the Cité des Sciences (a permanent educational exhibition complex built on the site of the former abattoirs at La Villette), I picked up a book by (Professor) *Jean-Marie Pelt … president of the European Ecological Institute. Published last year,* Fleurs, Fêtes et Saisons [Flowers, Feasts and Seasons] *certainly suggests that Europe is into plant lore and plant history.*

Re 1989: would you like me to 'do' this year's Burnley Expo?

Also, I have been following the development of the
new Visitor Centre at the Royal Botanic Gardens ...
(they) *do not want publicity until the full auditorium*
complex is complete. Certainly I think it is worth
describing. Would you like me to work on it?

As I said – lively, energetic, erudite. And involved. No editor could ask for more!

It is wonderful that Helen Forgasz, a former colleague, has sought out, collated and re-presented Nina Crone's journalistic output for *The Age* over a period of sixteen years. It is the usual fate of newspaper articles to be read, enjoyed, perhaps mulled over but then discarded and forgotten. Helen's initiative ensures that Nina's work lives on, not only for permanent enjoyment but for reference. I suspect this would have delighted its modest author.

Melbourne, May 2008

Preface

There are many people to thank for their support in the
production of this collection.

I am most grateful to the late Nina Crone for her fascinating
writings. I admire her dedication to the pursuit of her passion
while employed in the demanding position of principal at
Melbourne Girls Grammar School. No doubt the meticulous
research she undertook and the field trips and international
travel she clearly enjoyed provided an element of balance in an
otherwise relentless, and sometimes lonely, working life.
Freedom was something Nina cherished, and she was wise
enough not to allow her vocation to enmesh her life completely.

Nina's family, in particular her siblings Eleanor Leigh, and
John and Graeme Crone, enthusiastically embraced this project.
They gave copyright clearance to reproduce Nina's work, filled
many gaps in the Nina 'story', and located and passed on several
photographs taken by Nina that have been included in this book.
We have forged a friendship that will extend beyond the time
spent on this enterprise.

My sincerest thanks are extended to Melbourne Girls
Grammar School (MGGS) for supporting this project financially
and for facilitating the sale and distribution of the book. All
proceeds will go directly to the school and the monies will be
used to establish an academic prize in the name of Nina Alison
Crone. I am also grateful to the school for allowing the
exploration of the archives. Useful information on Nina during
her time as principal was located. Photographs and other
materials, including extracts from Nina's travel diaries,
personalise and contextualise Nina's published work and have
been included in the book.

The Old Grammarians Society of MGGS has also been most

supportive of the project, both financially and in kind. It was indeed an honour to launch the book at the Old Grammarians' function on 16 August 2008 in memory of Nina, to which all former students and staff from the 'Nina era' had been invited.

I am grateful to the Australian Garden History Society (AGHS) for its financial support of the book and for allowing archival materials to be reproduced in the book. It was through the AGHS that I was introduced to Helen Botham, who knew Nina as one of its active members and as editor of the society's journal, *Australian Garden History*. I could not have completed this project without Helen's assistance, knowledge of garden history and plants, and skills in identifying appropriate illustrations and photographs, including her own, to accompany many of Nina's articles.

Anne Latreille was another vital contributor to the project. She was the editor of the Gardening section of *The Age* during most of the time Nina contributed articles. She lent me her collection of clippings from *The Age*, enabling a fast search to identify those of Nina's articles that I did not have. In recognition of her role as Nina's editor, I invited Anne to write the foreword to the book, for which I thank her.

To complete the search for Nina's articles in *The Age*, microfilm (held at the Matheson Library, Monash University) was searched. Louise Hamilton meticulously trawled through the microfilm as far back as 1982 (when T. M. Garnett was editor of the Gardening section). As a consequence of Louise's efforts, I am confident that the collection of Nina's journalistic efforts found in these pages is complete. The Faculty of Education, Monash University, provided a small grant to enable this work to be carried out.

I am most appreciative of the artistic talents of Cam Knuckey. Several of Nina's articles in *The Age* were complemented by his illustrations. These, together with some new ones that Cam was invited to draw, have been included in this book.

My thanks are also extended to two other illustrators of

Nina's contributions in *The Age*, Richard Barley and Anita Podwyszynski, who allowed their drawings to be reproduced.

Jen Perry, a talented Melbourne artist, painted the image of Nina used on the front cover of the book. Her ability to capture and reproduce the essential Nina so masterfully, based only on photographic images, is remarkable.

Thanks are also due to Glenda Romeril, a friend and former colleague at MGGS, whose whimsical sketches accompany some of the articles included in this collection.

Fortunately for all, Nina Crone rarely threw anything out. Amongst her effects, her sister Eleanor found copies of the correspondence between Nina and the two editors of the gardening section of *The Age* with whom she had worked. Also located was a collection of previously unpublished articles, some of which had been submitted to *The Age* but had not appeared in the paper for various reasons. I am indebted to Brenda Joyce, another former MGGS colleague, whose literary talents and expertise were called upon to decide which of Nina's unpublished works should be included in this book. Brenda also assisted with the editing and proof-reading of the entire manuscript.

I sincerely thank Nick Walker of Australian Scholarly Publishing P/L for recognising the significance of Nina's writings. Thanks, too, to his staff for assisting with the layout and design.

To everyone who encouraged me to pursue this project and to those who provided background material to fill gaps and round out Nina's life story I am also most grateful.

Helen Forgasz
Melbourne, April 2008

Acknowledgements

Nina Crone's siblings – Graeme Crone, John Crone, and Eleanor Leigh – gave permission for the collection of articles authored by Alison Dalrymple (Nina Crone's pseudonym) and Nina Crone that had previously been published in The Age to be reproduced in this book. The Age has acknowledged the Crone family's permission. The Crone family also allowed a number of previously unpublished articles to be included.

On Nina's passing, the Crone family donated documents and photographic materials to the archives of Melbourne Girls Grammar School and the Australian Garden History Society. Both organisations have kindly permitted the reproduction of various photographs and other materials.

Botanic illustrators Cam Knuckey, Richard Barley, and Anita Podwyszynski, and sketch artist Glenda Romeril gave permission for their illustrations to be reproduced.

The front cover portrait of Nina Crone is the work of Melbourne artist, Jen Perry, who granted permission for it to be reproduced here and for all advertising materials.

The permissions of all other copyright owners whose images have been reproduced are acknowledged where the images are found in the book.

Helen Forgasz is an Associate Professor in the Faculty of Education, Monash University. Her main research interests are mathematics education and gender issues. Before embarking on doctoral studies and moving into academia, Helen was a teacher of mathematics and physics. She worked at Melbourne Girls Grammar School for seven years (1983 to 1989) during Nina Crone's time as principal.

Introduction

HELEN FORGASZ

A tribute to Nina Crone, gardening writer for *The Age*

The hand of history and the power of place exert
considerable influence in shaping the character of an
individual and determining the direction of his or her
life. (Nina Crone, 2004, p. 70)[1]

Nina Crone was a remarkable woman who lived a full and productive life. She began her professional career as a teacher, moved to the Australian Broadcasting Commission (ABC) (now Corporation) as a radio and television director and producer of children's educational programs and, for twenty years before her retirement at the end of 1994, was the principal of Melbourne Girls Grammar School (MGGS). Nina also had a passion for writing.

In this book, the collection of Nina Crone's writings about plants and gardens that were published between 1982 and 1997 in the pre-eminent Victorian newspaper, *The Age*, are reproduced. Also included are several previously unpublished manuscripts that were identified by her sister Eleanor as she sifted through Nina's possessions following her death. This collection serves as a tribute to the life of an extraordinary and complex woman, and as a mark of my respect for her as a former colleague and dear friend.

---

1 Crone, N. (2004). 'Becoming Australian'. In P. Alexander, J. Blakey, J. Harley, and E. Marshall (eds), *Out of Yesterday: Reflections on Our Australian Heritage*. Melbourne: Grey Thrush Publishing.

1

As nearly all of the articles in *The Age* were written under the pseudonym, Alison Dalrymple (Alison was Nina's middle name, and Dalrymple a family name), many who knew and worked with Nina may not have been aware that she wrote regularly for the Gardening section. Anne Latreille, the editor of the Gardening section of *The Age* for most of the time Nina contributed articles (1986–97) told me that she inherited the 'mysterious' Alison Dalrymple when she took over the editorship from T. M. (Tommy) Garnett. Having found out that Nina was writing under a pseudonym, Anne tried for many years to get her to write under her own name. This did not happen until 1997, when the last two articles that Nina wrote for *The Age* were published.

Reasons for using a pseudonym are not difficult to surmise. Since Nina was the principal of MGGS for most of the period of her journalistic endeavours with *The Age*, a *nom de plume* provided cover from the confines, scrutiny and critique of the school community. That it took two years after retirement for her to emerge and write under her own name may be indicative of the time it took to break free of the 'principal' label and the expectations surrounding it. On the other hand, by publishing under her own name she may also have been celebrating the receipt of her journalist's 'ticket', a course she completed in 1995, the year following her retirement.

I first met Nina in 1982 when she interviewed me for a teaching position at MGGS (at that time it was still known as the Melbourne Church of England Girls Grammar School or MCEGGS). I had seen an advertisement for a Mathematics and Physics teacher and sent in a cheeky application. It included a photograph of me and my science teacher colleagues taken during *Science Week*, an activity organised to promote girls' participation in Mathematics and Science[2] in the school where I worked. In the photograph, I wore a t-shirt with the words 'I'm a live wire, I'm a physicist'. For what I thought to be a stuffy and

---

2 The 1980s was an exciting decade for educators. Society's attitudes to women were being challenged and there was much activity aimed at breaking the male stereotype engulfing the fields of Mathematics and Science.

rather traditional school, I wanted the principal to know exactly what she would be getting if she were to appoint me. Unbeknown to me, Nina was herself a committed feminist and undoubtedly quickly deciphered my intent. I was a little surprised when, at 8 pm two days after sending the application, I received a phone call from her. What principal rings to organise a job interview, and at 8pm? I arrived for the interview at 4.30 pm the next day and was offered the job before I had left the room. I was overwhelmed by the charm, intellect, warmth and breadth of conversation of the person who had interviewed me. I couldn't believe how lucky I was to have been chosen to work in the school led by this woman.

During the seven years I taught at MGGS I learnt much about Nina Crone. An astute and volatile individual, she was a quick thinker, demanding, had high expectations, and was intolerant of foolishness. All recognised that her job was relentless and challenging. No one was indifferent towards her. But there was also a mischievous, fun-loving aspect to her personality. Nina was a regular at Happy Hour on Friday afternoons. After a couple of glasses, and with a twinkle in her eyes, Nina would regale those present with stories of the week's happenings. She liked naughty girls and revelled in taking the 'What would I do if it were me' approach to solving school-based 'crimes'.

I found out that Nina was writing for *The Age* not long after she asked if my daughters, then aged eleven and eight, would enjoy a visit to the 1986 Garden Show, held at Burnley in Melbourne. I was sure they would be delighted and told her so. One Saturday morning, I dropped the girls off at her house on the school premises. She brought them home in the afternoon and they could not stop talking about what they had seen and done. A few days later, I spotted an article in *The Age* (18 March) with the headline, 'Delight and inspiration at Garden Week 1986'. I perused the article, wondering if what was written would match with what the girls had told me. Just over halfway through I read:

Because publicity for Garden Week described it as 'an
invaluable exhibition for garden lovers and enthusiasts
of all ages', I took sixth-grader Rebecca and her younger
sister Rachel to Burnley.

It had to be more than a co-incidence that my daughters' names
had been used in the article – but it had been written by
someone named Alison Dalrymple, a name I certainly did not
know. I suspected she must be a friend of Nina's. The following
day at work I caught up with Nina and asked about the article
and its author. She admitted that she was Alison Dalrymple and
that she had been writing for *The Age* for some time. Much later
I learnt that, as a form of relaxation from the demands of her
job, Nina set herself the goal of writing an article within a self-
imposed deadline of two to three hours on a Saturday morning.

I began looking at the Gardening section of *The Age*
regularly to follow what Nina wrote. I remember challenging her
about the content of one article (17 June 1986). In it, she had
claimed that the pomegranate was a major contender as the fruit
of the 'Tree of Knowledge' in the biblical Garden of Eden story.
In a note to her, I explained that she had ignored Judaic sources
in which she would find that the fig was considered the most
likely candidate. Almost a year later (14 April 1987), an article on
the fig appeared in *The Age*. The opening sentence read:

My friend Helen has offered more contenders for Eden's
'Tree of Knowledge' and she has taken me to task for
neglecting Judaic commentaries in my account of the
pomegranate.

Close inspection of the collection of 'Plants in History' articles
that Nina wrote for *The Age* reveals her life interests and
passions: plants and gardens, history, all things French, human
relationships, and education. The plants at the focus of the
articles would be familiar to most, but the stories surrounding
them would not. Young and old, those interested or not in things
botanical can only be fascinated by the intertwining of the

botanical background of the plants and the intriguing historical contexts and facts related to them. Nina, the quintessential educator, is clearly apparent.

Nina was an intrepid traveller and in another series of articles she focuses on the many gardens in Australia and around the world that she visited. She was a serious diarist and her travel diaries, now archived at MGGS, provide detailed daily accounts of when she travelled, where she went, what she did, and what she saw. When the newspaper articles and the travel diaries are looked at simultaneously, it is very clear that her journalistic efforts were based on the entries in her diaries.

As well as revealing Nina's interests, the articles in *The Age* over the sixteen years of her writing (1982–97) reflect critical phases in her life. There can be little doubt that the period 1984–90, the years of the bulk of her writing for *The Age*, was a stable time both professionally and personally. Having commenced as principal of MGGS in 1975, she was now well-ensconced in the role. She had also established herself as a leader among the principals of the independent schools in Victoria and across Australia. In 1985, she was the chair of the Association of Heads of Independent Girls Schools in Victoria. As noted in the constitution of the Association of Heads of Independent Schools of Australia (AHISA), she was a member of the inaugural Standing Committee of that association, also founded in 1985 when the Headmasters' Conference of the Independent Schools of Australia (HMC) and the Association of Heads of Independent Girls' Schools of Australia (AHIGSA) joined forces.

There was a five-year hiatus, mid-1990 to mid-1995, in which no articles appeared in *The Age*. The last article before the break was published on 5 June 1990 and was about the aubergine. In it, Nina wrote of turning to her sister, Eleanor, for guidance on plantings that would cope with the 'land recently cleared of swamp paperbark (*Melaleuca squarrosa*), incipient bracken, poor drainage, heavy soil, tank water and intermittent settlement'. This was the block of land in Walkerville that Nina had cleared herself, and where she built the house she would retire to and live in for ten years. It was at Walkerville that she designed and planted a magnificent garden that was central to some of her later writings, including a few published in *The Age* and included in this book.

Those five years coincided with the time that Nina's professional career as principal of MGGS came to an end. The period was particularly turbulent for the school. It was also undoubtedly demanding and stressful, besieging her time to write. In 1991, Melbourne Grammar School (the 'brother' school of MGGS) declared a move to co-education. Luke Slattery (*The Age*, 10 December 1991, p. 13) wrote that the 'decision carries immense symbolic weight' and that:

> *Melbourne Girls' Grammar is the school most likely to be [sic] feel the immediate impact of Melbourne Grammar's decision, as the families most likely to send their children to these most elite of private schools now have a coeducation option. Yet the principal, Miss Nina Crone, is unperturbed, feeling that the two schools will continue to cooperate where they can. Nor does she feel her school's enrolments are under threat.*

There was talk of the two schools merging, a move successfully opposed by Nina and the School Council. In early 2007, when invited back to the school to speak to Year 7 students undertaking a project on her time as principal, Nina admitted that she believed that a takeover had been the intention and that, in her view, the girls and the staff of MGGS would have been the losers had it eventuated. Pressure to gain parental support against the amalgamation of the two schools must have been intense and demanding.

In 1992, Nina wrote a letter to the editor of *The Age* (19 September 1992, p. 10) outlining drawbacks in the International Baccalaureate (IB) as a substitute for the local Victorian Certificate of Education (VCE) as a means of university entrance for Victorian students. She wrote:

While students, parents and schools have grown
justifiably weary of the VCE being politicised, before
deserting it for an international product we should first
consider the only question which matters. This is, what
best meets the needs of Australian students, remembering
some will want an international educational passport
and all need a certificate respected for its credible
assessment.

At that time, competition for enrolments in independent schools was fierce and the IB had been introduced by several competitors. It is likely that there were demands from some that MGGS follow this trend, a move, it seems, that Nina opposed.

In 1993, the centenary of MGGS occurred. Several celebratory functions and events were included in the school calendar. In *The Age* of 10 June 1993 (p. 13), John Lahey reported on a paper presented by Nina at the Centenary Dinner. In it, she recounted the tragic love story of the Liets. The topic was an appropriate one for the school's centenary celebration as it was Madame Liet who had taught the first French lesson at the school. Madame Liet's life became the focus of Nina's writing a decade later. In a diary entry from 8 September 2005, Nina describes a visit to 'see the Liet papers'. She wrote that there were 'far more than I imagined' and referred to her correspondence about them twelve years earlier. From late 2005, following a period as editor of the *Australian Garden History*, Nina put much effort into researching and writing Madame Liet's biography. It was near completion when she died. Her family has planned that the biography be completed posthumously.

While there is no apparent indicator for the lack of articles in *The Age* during 1994, it was the last year of Nina's term as principal. Perhaps her spare time was taken up preparing for her retirement. Once she had moved and had settled in to her Walkerville home, she resumed writing for *The Age*. The first article, 'Venus by the sea', appeared on 28 October 1995 and featured the Kitchen Garden at Venus Bay in Gippsland, not far from her home in Walkerville. From 1995 to 1997, Nina only wrote sporadically for *The Age*. Her interests had begun to shift. As evidenced by the articles in *The Age* during that period, Gippsland was becoming a focus for her writing as well as her community involvements. She was also returning to writing about the history of gardens and their place in people's lives, rather than on individual plants. The penultimate article in *The Age* was about her own garden, and was written under her own name. The light-hearted Nina shone through:

> *After Operation Clean-up, Cover-up and Conserve Water,*
> *I can put down my rake and add plenty of ice to the*
> *drinks with a clear conscience.*

Nina's last article in *The Age* was a review of a book on the Rothschild family's gardens (12 April 1997) in which the history of the disruption to their lives, through wars and the Nazi regime, was also described.

When Nina stopped writing for *The Age*, a new phase of her writing life had already begun. She was contributing articles to *Australian Garden History*, the journal of the Australian Garden History Society (AGHS). The first was entitled 'Autumnal wanderings. Pre-conference tour',[3] and appeared in the July–August issue of 1997. An interesting note at the conclusion of the article revealed Nina's long-kept garden writing secret:

> *As a free-lance garden writer, Nina Crone has written*
> *for The Age under the name of Alison Dalrymple for 15*
> *years. She says her interest in gardening was*
> *subconsciously stimulated by being educated opposite*
> *Melbourne's Fitzroy Gardens (at PLC in East Melbourne)*
> *and by working for twenty years opposite the Royal*
> *Botanic Gardens (at MGGS). (p. 18)*

Nina was to become editor of *Australian Garden History* for five

---

3 Crone, N. (1997). 'Autumnal wanderings. Pre-conference tour'. *Australian Garden History*, 9(1), 16–18.

years until May–June 2006. From 1997 until her death in 2007 she also wrote many articles for the journal, contributed a chapter in the book *Planting the Nation*,[4] and was an active member of the AGHS. A moving tribute to Nina's involvement in the AGHS, and examples of her early writing which comprise part of the entire collection reproduced here, were found in the September–October 2007 issue of *Australian Garden History*.

In the last decade of her life, Nina's writing skills extended beyond her involvement with *Australian Garden History*. She was a member of the Writers' Circle of the Lyceum Club in Melbourne and contributed an essay, 'Becoming Australian', to a volume entitled *Out of Yesterday*; the quote at the beginning of this introduction was taken from Nina's article. Among her other pursuits, she chaired school councils, assisted former colleagues and friends in need, and was a lively and entertaining guide at the Johnston Collection, a museum dedicated to the fine and decorative arts situated in East Melbourne, near the home she returned to after her time in Walkerville.

Nina Crone led an active and creative life. Writing was a passion as, too, was the history of gardens and plants, the central theme of most of her writing. In 1975, her first year as principal of MGGS, her contribution in the school magazine reflected her life-long respect for the written word:

> *Ideas are shared and effectively communicated through words and pictures … The craft of words, like any other craft, demands the integrity, the imagination, the skill which characterize the work of an artisan …*

I remained friends with Nina from the time I first met her at that interview for the job at MGGS in 1982 until her untimely death on 14 July 2007, Bastille Day. Nina left this world too soon. I miss her.

---

4 Crone, N. (2001). 'Symbols of a new nation: Australia's flora in the decorative arts 1890–1914'. In G. Whitehead (ed.), *Planting the Nation* (pp. 75–93). Melbourne: Australian Garden History Society.

The origins of Nina's writings on gardens and plants

There would appear to be two different beginnings to Nina's journalistic endeavours in *The Age*. Both are related to her work at Melbourne Girls Grammar School.

In 1981, Nina taught American History to a class of year 11 girls. A copy of a leaflet entitled 'American trees in the Royal Botanic Gardens, Melbourne', was found in one of her files, and the front page of the eight-page leaflet is reproduced below. It seems that the leaflet was the product of a project undertaken by the American History class. As indicated on the front page, the American Tree Trail described had been designed for visitors to the Royal Botanic Gardens, Melbourne. The route through the gardens to encounter American trees and plants is outlined in the booklet and descriptions of the flora and their roles in American history are provided.

Using the pseudonym Alison Dalrymple, Nina wrote to the Gardening editor of *The Age* on 18 June 1982:

> *I submit two articles for your consideration and possible use in the gardening section of The Age 'Weekender' during the [International] Year of the Tree.*

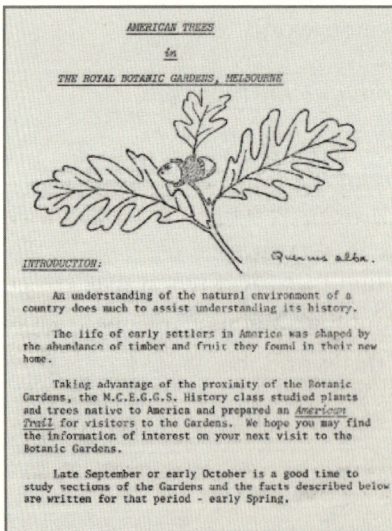

Front page of a leaflet produced by Nina Crone's American History class of 1981.

One of the two articles was 'The American Tree Trail', the very first of Nina's articles to be published in *The Age*, on 8 October 1982. The contents of that article were very clearly aligned to the material included in the 'American trees in the Royal Botanic Gardens, Melbourne' leaflet. Nina's comments in the school magazine of 1982 reflect the significance to her at that time of the links between the school, the International Year of the Tree, and the Royal Botanic Gardens, Melbourne:

*The International Year of the Tree highlights the unique
location of this school. Few schools in the world lie
opposite gardens of international reputation. MCEGGS
uses the Royal Botanic Gardens in many ways – for art
classes, biology and science classes, history classes,
creative writing groups and Year 12 girls lunch there.*

The second article Nina submitted for consideration for
publication in *The Age* was 'The Douglas Fir'. In his letter of
reply (dated 26 August 1982), Tommy Garnett commented that
he had himself recently written an article about David Douglas,
after whom the tree was named, and so would keep Nina's
article aside for a later date. The article was never published, but
has been included in this collection.

No more of Nina's articles were published in *The Age* until 24
August 1984 when 'A world of contrasts waits in the Big Apple',
about the Brooklyn Botanical Gardens in New York, appeared.
This article represented a second beginning for Nina's writings
for *The Age*. Its genesis was an earlier visit to New York City.

In a draft of a talk to the Friends of the Geelong Botanic
Gardens (dated Monday 23 August 2004), Nina described the
origins of her interest in public gardens and her early writings
for *The Age* as follows:

*In the late summer of 1984[5] I was in New York. I had
visited the Guggenheim, the World Trade Centre, the
United Nations Building, the Statue of Liberty and Staten
Island. The steam issuing from the pavement gratings
and the shark-like cabs cruising the streets in the
canyons of Manhattan were fascinating icons of a city
like no other that I had experienced. I was tired of the
conference venues with no outlook to the exterior world
and of schools in sky scrapers with no open space for*

---

5 Nina probably made a mistake with the date, 1984. What is written about New
   York and the Brooklyn Botanic Gardens in this talk for the Geelong Friends of the
   Botanic Gardens matches her travel diary entries for August 1980.

*recreation. I took the subway to Brooklyn and walked to
the Botanic Gardens. They were a revelation and marked
a pivotal moment in determining the use of free time
while on business trips. For the next decade whenever I
was in an overseas city I sought the public gardens.*

*Back in Melbourne I wrote about them for Tommy
Garnett's page in The Age and I began visiting as many
private gardens throughout Australia as I could fit into a
busy professional life. The aspect of the gardens, both
public and private, that particularly appealed to me was
their history – their evolution, their makers, and the
influences on them.*

Clearly inspired by what she had seen and experienced in New
York, Nina began writing in earnest about gardens she had
visited around the world and in Australia. The articles were
clearly targeted for the readership of *The Age*. On 28 July 1984,
she wrote to Tommy Garnett:

*Do you think an occasional series, representing the
current state of public gardens, interstate and overseas,
would generate interest and focus attention on different
ways of involving people in their city's parks? To illustrate
what I had in mind, I enclose three pieces on botanic
gardens in different places.*

On 7 August 1984, Tommy Garnett replied:

*Thank-you for the latest (extremely professionally-
presented) trio. I shall hope to use all of them – probably
at intervals of once a month, and beginning with the one
on the BBG [Brooklyn Botanic Gardens – the article was
published in The Age on 24 August 1984].*

Thus began a further fourteen-year (1984–97) writing period for
The Age. In all, Nina wrote seventy articles using her *nom de
plume* and two, the last she wrote, were published in 1997 under
her own name.

The structure and content of this book

This book is a tribute to my friend Nina Crone and to her creative endeavours, her passions, her perspectives on flora, and on the contributions gardens and plants have made to the well-being of humanity and the world.

Putting the book together has been a way for me to come to terms with Nina's untimely passing. She touched the lives of countless Australians through her early work as a teacher, as a director and producer for children's radio and television programs for the ABC, as principal of Melbourne Girls Grammar School, and as a member of a vast range of professional and voluntary organisations and committees. Using the pseudonym Alison Dalrymple, she also educated and entertained many with her writings about gardens and plants in *The Age* newspaper.

Nina's actions and words were consistent with her belief that it was people's worldly experiences and passions that turned them into interesting and creative individuals, as well as inspiring educators. Her semi-covert journalistic exploits during her time as principal of MGGS hinted at other dimensions to her persona that would have been hidden from many who only knew her in the school context. The MGGS community should know that Nina Crone was more than just their principal, teacher, colleague or boss. The topics she selected to write about, and the themes that emerged, paralleled her lived interests, passions and concerns. These were factors that inspired me to put this collection together.

In this book, the entire collection of articles from *The Age,* and a selection of previously unpublished articles, have been clustered into three groupings:

* *Plants.* The articles here focus on one or more individual plants. The histories of the plants as well as their roles in the shaping of the human condition are recounted.
* *Gardens.* The ambience of many public gardens and spaces beyond Victoria and the botanical significance of the plants found in these locations are highlighted in this collection of articles.

*   *Close to home.* These articles centre on flora and their contributions to the life of Melbourne and the Gippsland region of Victoria, Nina's homes at various times between 1982 and 1997. A few articles that did not fit well into the other categories, and which characterise Nina, the instinctive educator, have also been included.

Introductory comments precede each group of articles, and the articles are presented in chronological order of publication in *The Age*; previously unpublished works are found at the end of each pertinent cluster. The vast majority of articles are accompanied by photographs or illustrations. Much of the artwork was created by Cam Knuckey, one of the illustrators of several of Nina's original articles in *The Age*. Also included is the work of two other botanical illustrators from *The Age*: Anita Podwyszynski and Richard Barley, current Director of the Royal Botanic Gardens, Melbourne, who has family links to the early history of Melbourne Girls Grammar School through his great grandfather, William Morris, and great-aunts, Mary and Edith Morris. Other sketches were provided by Glenda Romeril, a former colleague from MGGS.

Many of the photographs included in the book were taken by Nina on her adventures and travels and now reside in the archives of MGGS or the Australian Garden History Society. It was not always clear exactly when Nina's photographs were taken, but there can be no doubt that in each case it was prior to the date of publication of the related article in *The Age*. Other photographs and illustrations were gleaned from a variety of sources; relevant dates and origins are clearly indicated in the accompanying captions.

It is my wish that all who read the articles in this volume will enjoy them and will learn something about the world of plants, gardens, and their relationship to humankind, as expressed through the pen of a talented and unique woman, Nina Crone.

Editorial issues

Inevitably, there were a few spelling and typographical errors in the articles originally published in *The Age*. These have been corrected, rather that using 'sic' in the text to identify them.

In consultation with horticultural experts, minor (mainly spelling) corrections have also been made to botanical names.

In *The Age* articles, American spellings for words such as 'color', 'flavor' etc. were used; these have been retained throughout. Less common spellings of some words such as 'wistaria' (for the more familiar 'wisteria') have also been left unchanged.

Some of the articles in *The Age* were untitled. Simple titles, to guide the reader as to the theme or main focus of each article, have been provided. It is clearly indicated where this has occurred.

Photographers, or sources of photographs for which permissions were obtained, are acknowledged together with the pertinent photographs.

Plants

Plants: introduction

Most of the articles included in this section of the book are from the 'Plants in History' series published in *The Age*. When Nina Crone conceived the idea for the series, she wrote to Anne Latreille, the editor of the Gardening section at the time, and enclosed samples of what she had in mind. In her letter, she added that 'it would be most distinguished if Cam Knuckey ... could illustrate the subject!' Several of the articles published in *The Age* were illustrated by Cam. In recognition of Nina's admiration for his work, Cam was commissioned to illustrate the majority of the contributions included here.

Articles in the same genre as the 'Plants in History' series are also found in this section. Their focus is on individual plants, or sometimes a group of related plants. Botanical information is accompanied by accounts – factual or mythical – of the place of these plants in the natural world, their roles in shaping human history, or their effects on human relationships.

The plants Nina wrote about would be familiar to most and included a range of fruits and vegetables, various trees and shrubs, and many flowers.

Strong, common themes are clearly evident in the collection. Several articles reflect a religious or spiritual dimension: Christianity, including Christmas and Easter; Judaism; Buddhism; and Islam. People and places from around the globe feature, and Nina's love for all things French and for Australia is quite obvious. Tales, legends, anecdotes and historical fact are communicated and, at times, Nina delves into the highs and lows of human intrigue, sensitivities and emotions. Whether tragic, romantic, gruesome or uplifting, the narratives stir and satisfy the reader's curiosity, adding spice and context to factual knowledge of the featured botanical species. Snippets of Nina's personal life, stretching back to her early years, her travels, her family and her friends, can be discerned in several articles.

Remarkably well researched and skilfully written, these articles will stimulate interest, entertain and educate.

Helen Forgasz

Setting a fashion for violets

The floral preferences of today's political leaders have not been revealed – at least not publicly. It was different last century, when Napoleon Bonaparte set a fashion for violets.

Leaving for exile on the island of Elba, Napoleon assured his supporters that he 'would return with the violets in spring'. Bonapartists immediately adopted his favorite flower as their symbol and password. It featured on stationery, on crockery, on jewellery. The toast was 'To Corporal Violet in the spring'.

And return he did in 1815, greeted everywhere by violets. The cult survived the Bourbon restoration to such an extent that in 1879 200 tons of violets were harvested in a single region of the Riviera.

Viola odorata was also popular in Victorian England where the coy and cloying couplet –

Roses are red, violets are blue,
Honey is sweet, and so are you

appeared in many turn-of the-century autograph books.

The Age, 11 March 1986, p. 31.

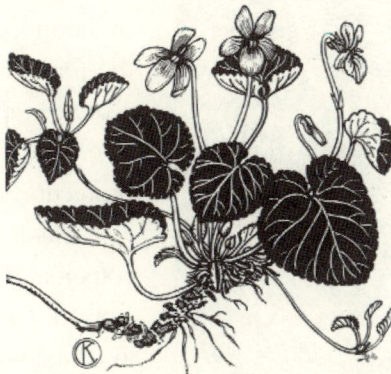

The cabbage[*]

Boiled cabbage in bed-sitters along Gloucester Road, the ceremonial pomp of a coronation and the triumph of Everest conquered are the incongruous memories of a working holiday in London in the 1950s.

The cabbage (*Brassica oleracea*) is so much part of English food lore that the French say: 'The English have three vegetables – two of them are cabbage!'

For a sea-faring people, the cabbage had an essential place in every ship's galley if scurvy was to be contained. Loads of the ubiquitous vegetable trundled from commercial plots in Battersea to the market at Covent Garden, or were barged downstream to Wapping and Greenwich.

Long before the Romans introduced it to Britain, the cabbage held a respected place in ancient civilisations. The Egyptians worshipped it and that thoughtful Greek, Pythagoras, extolled its many qualities. Greeks and Romans included pickled and spiced cabbage on their banquet menus.

Centuries later the English cottagers grew cabbages and respected a tradition that, when cutting it, the remaining stalk should be scored in the form of a cross to ensure new growth and protection from the devil.

Was it, I wonder, the cottagers who started the story of babies being found in cabbages? When you

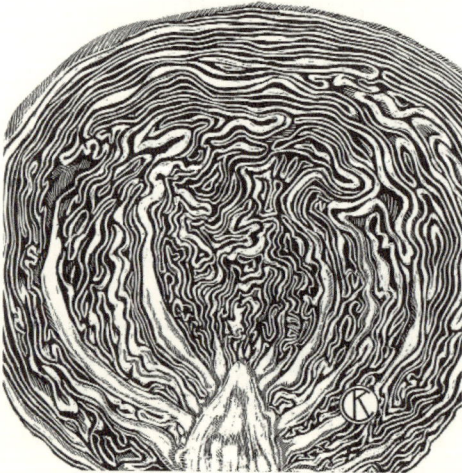

consider that a Nottingham garden produced an 18-kilogram cabbage in 1966, the story is not so improbable.

The Germans made the cabbage their own in sauerkraut, the Russians put it into borscht, the Chinese grew their own special variety, and I feel sure dehydrated cabbage journeys into space.

As for the French, in practice they are not so disdainful of this useful plant. When Louis XIV suggested to Le Nôtre, his famous garden designer, that he should have a coat-of-arms, Le Nôtre declined, saying he already had one – 'Three slugs surrounding a spade, crowned with cabbage leaves'.

Isn't that right, *mon petit chou?*

The Age, Tuesday 15 April 1986, Home, p. 6.
* title provided by HF

$\mathcal{D}$*israeli admired a humble flower*

The English Prime Minister, Benjamin Disraeli, chose the primrose as his favorite flower. When he died, a primrose wreath lay on his coffin. The flowers had come from the Queen's summer palace on the Isle of Wight. The handwritten card read:

> *His favorite flower from Osbourne. A tribute of affectionate regard from Queen Victoria.*

At the unveiling of a statue commemorating the great statesman, all the Tory members of Parliament wore a primrose in their buttonhole.

This custom became identified with the influential think-tank group in the Conservative Party – the Primrose League.

April 19, the anniversary of Disraeli's death, is celebrated each year by the distribution and wearing of the humble woodland flower.

The Age, 22 April 1986, p. 25.

The heath *

From April to November bushwalkers may find Victoria's floral emblem, *Epacris impressa* Labill (the common heath), in its native habitat. Close observation reveals the reason for the species' name – *impressa*. Each bell on the stem has five small dimples or 'impressions' surrounding its base. However, there is quite a story behind the abbreviation Labill which identifies the man who first described the specimen in 1805.

The French botanist Jacques-Julien Houton de Labillardière collected the species in Tasmania in 1793. He was aboard the ship (captained by Bruny d'Entrecasteaux) which was searching for the missing explorer La Pérouse. But before Labillardière could describe his find for scientific journals, the wake of the French Revolution reached Australian waters. D'Entrecasteaux died in July 1793 and royalist officers on the ships *La Recherche* and *L'Espérance* handed the specimens to England's allies, the Dutch, in Java.

Labillardière, a republican, was imprisoned in Java for 18 months and his

plant collection of more than 400 specimens went to England as war booty. Through the diplomatic intervention of Sir Joseph Banks, who ranked research above royalism or republicanism, the collection reached its rightful owner in France.

Victoria was the first Australian state to proclaim an official floral emblem. The College of Arms in London registered an addition to the Victorian coat of arms according to the heraldic description

> … *upon a Compartment of Grass, springing therefrom …*
> *a representation of the Floral Emblem of the said State of*
> *Victoria, that is to say, the Pink Form of the Common*
> *Heath, Epacris impressa Labill.*

The Age, 6 May 1986, p. 37.
* title provided by HF

The flavor of mythology

W hen I was young, my elders and betters exhorted: 'Look to your laurels, my girl!' I began to cultivate my laurel or bay-tree (*Laurus nobilis*) only when I sought respect through soups and sauces, stews and shasliks.

The bay leaf was a secret weapon in approaching the necessary chore of cooking as an art form. Add a bay leaf to your stockpot and you add the flavor of mythology and history.

The nymph Daphne, fleeing the amorous Apollo, thwarted his ardor by turning into a bay-tree. Sadly, Apollo gathered its leaves and wore them about his head, declaring that all who wished his favor should do likewise.

Thereafter, the Greeks rewarded accomplishment in battle,

sporting contests, literature or scholarship with a crown of laurel or bay leaves. This custom continued through history, and branches of bay, signifying victory, decorated the mail-coaches which took news of Wellington's triumph at Waterloo to the towns and villages of England.

Tradition also claimed that a flourishing bay-tree evidenced Apollo's favor and augured success for its owner. Conversely, if a bay-tree withered or died, it was an omen of impending disaster. Before the death of Nero, it is said, all the Roman bay-trees died.

Those who know their Shakespeare will recognise that superstition in the lines of *Richard II* (Act II, Scene IV):

'Tis thought the king is dead,
we will not stay,
The bay-trees in our country
are all withered away.

The Age, 27 May 1986, p. 27.

A sour yet sweet favorite

Debate and conjecture will continue forever over the fruit borne by the Tree of Knowledge in the Garden of Eden. Some people nominate the pomegranate, others the quince.

As far as the fruit is concerned, on aesthetic grounds I declare for the pomegranate, and it is pleasing to see it finding a place on fruiterers' counters.

In the Renaissance period the pomegranate became a popular subject for armorial bearings. Henri de Navarre (later Henri IV of France), whose kingdom bordered the Pyrenees, admired the Moorish culture of Granada where the pomegranate was a favorite fruit.

Henri took the pomegranate as his devise and his motto, 'Sour, yet sweet', referred to its distinctive flavor as much as to his political style.

A Spanish connection brought the pomegranate into English heraldry. Henry VIII's first wife, Catherine of Aragon, had the fruit as her emblem. Soon after her arrival in England a court masque in her honor featured displays of roses (for England) and pomegranates (for Spain). Catherine's daughter Mary adopted roses and pomegranates as her emblem.

Punica granatum was widely known in Mediterranean areas and the ancient Greeks claimed it originated from the blood of Dionysus, the god of wine. It was

also associated with Persephone, goddess of the underworld.

In plant lore the pomegranate is a fruit strongly associated with the female principle, which may account for my prejudice in favor of its claim to a place in Eden.

The Age, 17 June 1986, p. 23.

The chrysanthemum*

Of the tawny florist's chrysanthemums, the golden ginkgos and the fiery Japanese maples at the heart of autumn splendor in many countries, it is the chrysanthemum that dominates oriental plant lore.

It graced the Chinese imperial gardens more than 2500 years ago and then moved into Japan to become the Mikado's emblem, and, in stylised design, the national symbol.

A Chinese legend describes the origin of the chrysanthemum. A maiden asked a spirit how many years her coming marriage would last. 'As many years as there are petals on the flower of your wedding dress', was the reply.

The anxious girl searched everywhere but she found only five-petalled flowers. At last she discovered one with 17 petals, and, with her hairpin, she split each petal into two and then into four.

The prophecy came true. She

enjoyed 68 years of married life. Since then the chrysanthemum has been revered in the East as a symbol of purity and long life. Many oriental silks have a chrysanthemum design woven into them.

This 'golden flower' (*Chrysos anthos*) was reluctantly given to European plant collectors who often resorted to subterfuge to acquire it.

In the 1820s, John Reeves used his position as chief inspector of tea in Canton to export the flowers, while somewhat later, in Japan, the German eye-specialist, Philipp von Siebold, found medical practice a perfect cover for his trade in chrysanthemums.

By tradition the chrysanthemum represents abundance, regal beauty, truth, and cheerfulness in adversity. Few people presenting the white flowers on Mother's Day appreciate the symbolism of their bouquet.

The Age, 1 July 1986, p. 25.
* title provided by HF

Will Victoria's link with Venus prevail?

Will Sarah Ferguson continue a royal floral tradition when she marries Prince Andrew tomorrow?

Queen Victoria planted the myrtle sprig she had carried at her marriage to Prince Albert in 1840 in the garden of Osborne House on the Isle of Wight, and from that plant future royal brides took sprigs for bouquets. Queen Elizabeth II, Princess Margaret, Princess Anne and the Princess of Wales continued the custom.

The garden by the sea on the Isle of Wight was an

appropriate site for a plant associated with Venus, whose birthplace was the sea. Myth and iconography link Venus with the fragrant shrub *Myrtis communis.*

Venus took refuge behind a myrtle bush when satyrs discovered her bathing on the Island of Cytherea. She was wearing myrtle in her hair when Paris awarded her the golden apple on Mount Ida. So the myrtle became symbolic of love and beauty, and groves of it often surrounded temples dedicated to Venus.

Moslem tradition also acknowledges the myrtle and relates how Adam considered it the chief of all sweet-scented flowers. He took it with him when banished from the Garden of Eden, and thereafter it found a place in Persian and Moorish gardens.

When Greek immigrants sailed to establish new colonies they took boughs of myrtle with them to mark the close of an old life-style and the beginning of a new one.

If the bride carries myrtle in her bouquet for this reason, perhaps the bridegroom should also wear it in his buttonhole.

The Age, Tuesday 22 July 1986, Home, p. 5.

Pineapples polled well as a gift

There was a tradition in New England ports that sea captains gave a pineapple as thanks for hospitality received ashore. This custom led households willing to welcome seamen to signal the fact through an architectural logo. From New Haven through Narangansett, Newport and Nantucket, and north to Boston, Salem and Marblehead you can see pineapple motifs embellishing gateposts and finials.

The pineapple was a handy fruit for the sailor. It lasted well on a long voyage, it prevented scurvy and its exotic fragrance, flavor and appearance made it an impressive souvenir of tropical adventure.

Writing of his father's second voyage (to Guadeloupe), Ferdinand Columbus described '… fruits which look like our pinecones, but are much bigger; they are full of thick flesh like that of a melon, but of a much more delicate scent and flavor'.

The plant *Ananas sativus* is a native of Mexico, Panama, the upper Orinoco River area, Guyana and Brazil where it was called *nâna*.

Oviedo y Valdez, who discovered the pineapple in cultivation in Haiti in 1513, commended it to Ferdinand of Spain as an aid to digestion. Some time later Charles V of Spain was so suspicious of the strange fruit that he refused to eat it, fearing it to be poisoned.

By the 16th century the pineapple was aboard many ships plying world trade routes. It became familiar in ports of call and trading stations in India, South Africa and the islands of the Atlantic (the Canaries and the Azores) and the Pacific, particularly Hawaii.

The pineapple came to Britain during the 17th century. In 1661 John Evelyn described how King Charles II ate a Queen pineapple imported from the Barbados, adding that Cromwell had received some four years previously.

By the next century England was obsessed with endeavors to cultivate exotic plants. The pineapple was grown in the Chelsea Physic Garden where Georg Dionysius Ehret drew it for inclusion in *Plantae Selectae*, published by his German patron, Dr Trew.

Throughout England, pineapples were raised in the glasshouses of the aristocracy. At Stowe Hall in Berkshire in 1733, they were sold for half a guinea each.

Today, when unexpected visitors arrive, I reach for the can of pineapple that has a permanent place in my pantry. It may go into a planter's punch, an oriental sweet and sour, a tropical salad or a yeasty upside-down cake. The golden circle has come full round.

The Age, 12 August 1986, p. 26.

A symbol of undying love

Winter gillyflower sounds more romantic than wallflower and chevisance more exotic than either. But whatever name you choose to give it, *Cheiranthus cheiri* is known for its sweet scent.

A plant of Moorish origin, it is possible that Crusaders returning from Spain unwittingly brought seed with them and it settled in crevices and crannies of castle walls and battlements.

In such a castle during the 14th century lived Elizabeth, daughter of the Scottish Earl of March. She was betrothed to a prince but she loved the son of a border chieftain.

When her father locked her in the castle, her suitor, disguised as a minstrel, serenaded her from outside the castle wall. The lovers planned to elope and Elizabeth threw down a sprig of wallflower to encourage her minstrel.

Sadly, Elizabeth fell to her death while trying to escape from her turret and her mourning lover wandered Europe wearing the wallflower in his cap. Thereafter troubadors adopted the flower as a symbol of constancy in love as they sang their way from castle to castle across Europe.

The 17th century poet Robert Herrick introduced a new twist to the story when he wrote

Love in pity of the deed
And her Loving-luckless speed
Turned her to this plant we call
Now, the Flower of the Wall.

By Herrick's time, the wallflower was widely used by herbalists. It

was also an important flower for the husbandman because it attracted the bees and in some parts of England it was called the 'bee flower'.

Cottagers planted the wallflower outside their windows where the sweet fragrance wafted inside, bringing the romance of a mediaeval castle to a 19th century cottage.

The Age, 2 September 1986, p. 20.

Thanks to Turks for gift of tulips

Under Suleiman the Magnificent, Constantinople was reputed to be the most beautiful city in the world, and the tulip contributed to that reputation.

As the official flower of the sultan's court, the tulip was cultivated in breathtaking array in the extensive gardens of the summer palace at Adrianople (now Edirne) on the banks of the Maritsa River in European Turkey. When the sultan held his tulip festival at the Seraglio in Constantinople each year, exquisite vases overflowed with the most costly flowers.

The Turks strictly controlled the standard of the tulips, carefully recording all varieties in 'Ferahenzi', the oldest known tulip book. One grand vizier was given the name Lalizari – lover of tulips – for his work in publishing the *Mizanul Ezhar* which listed 1323 tulips and described varieties from Aleppo, Shiraz and Turkmenistan.

Entries in a tulip book conformed to rigorous standards. The flower had to resemble an almond, the shape of each petal had to resemble a dagger, the petals had to touch each other, the three innermost petals had to be narrower than the three outermost, the anthers and ovaries had to be hidden from sight, and so on.

Foreign representatives at the Ottoman court were the first to bring news of these beautiful flowers to Europe. A Belgian envoy of the German emperor sent tulip seeds to Clusius, who was working in Prague at the time.

After he moved to the 'Hortus' in Leiden, Clusius published facts about the tulip in 1575, although the German Conrad Gesner and Rembert Dodoen (Dodonaeus) had described the flower a decade earlier.

In England, Richard Hakluyt wrote of 'tulipas' imported from Austria, and John Parkinson included engravings of tulips in his *Paradisi in Sole* to complement his description of 'the turkes cap'.

The establishment of the Dutch East India Company in 1602 encouraged trade in tulip bulbs. Adrian Pauw, a director of the company, surrounded his house with 'a profusion of tulips clustered around a mirrored gazebo'. Among them was 'Semper Augustus', the fabulous tulip which flowered scarlet and white, flamed rose and changed hands for 5500 florins.

The Dutch promoted the tulip as a speculative commodity. At the height of 'tulipomania' (between 1634 and 1637) bulbs were exchanged for money, for pedigreed livestock or for real estate.

The masterly flower studies of Jan 'Velvet' Brueghel, and of Jan Van Huysum who painted tulips from the fields of Haarlem, helped maintain world interest in the Dutch bulb industry.

The English gardener, Sir Thomas Hanmer, was swept up in the enthusiasm. He wrote in his *Garden Book* of 'the Queen of bulbous plants whose flower is most beautiful in its figure and most rich and admirable in color and wonderful in variety of markings'.

The tulip was also John Rea's favorite and the one which most delighted him was 'Agate Hanmer', Sir Thomas's great triumph – 'a beautiful flower of three good colors – pale grideline, deep scarlet and pure white commonly well parted, striped, agated'.

But floral fashion is as fickle as any other. For wealthy European plant fanciers the exotic offerings of 18th century collectors working in Africa, Asia, the Americas and the Pacific soon superseded the tulip.

But the gardens of the emerging American estates – the Van Cortlandts at Croton-on-Hudson, of George Mason near Williamsburg, of Jefferson at Monticello and Washington at Mount Vernon – inherited the love of tulips.

At the same time in England the tulip was taking its place among the florists' flowers, brightening the drab lives of factory workers 'who [tended] their flowers themselves and watched over their progress with paternal solicitude'. But, because of its cost, the tulip was never as popular as the pink or auricula.

As we revel in our colorful tulip crop remember that always, everywhere, tulips remain (in Vita Sackville-West's words):

Alien Asiatics that have blown
Between the boulders of the Persian hill
Long centuries before they reached the dykes
To charm Van Huysum and the curious Breughel.

The Age, 30 September 1986, Home, p. 4.

The tree of Circe,
the sorceress, still gives magic

A weeping willow (*Salix babylonica*) stands to the west of Eel Bridge in the Royal Botanic Gardens. It was raised from a cutting taken from a willow growing beside Napoleon's grave.

'Napoleon' willows were the fashion among trendy 19th century gardeners who had little worry about stringent plant quarantine. Garden historian Miles Hadfield describes how Mrs Lawrence of Drayton Green set her Napoleon willow beside 'a fountain with its basin full of water lilies'.

Wood from the white willow (*S. alba*) has provided cricket bats for generations of aspiring Test players, while basket-makers sought the pliant withys of the osier beds for their traditional craft and the furry catkins of the pussy willow (*S. caprea*) have stirred the imagination of countless children.

Like the cypress, the willow is associated with sadness and death. In mythology it was sacred to Circe, Hecate and Persephone who each represented the dark side of experience.

In Judaic culture, willow branches were gathered to celebrate the Feast of the Tabernacles. It was on the willows that the exiled Jews

hung their harps when they sat down beside the waters of
Babylon to remember Zion.

Last century, American horticulturist and landscape designer
Andrew Jackson Downing felt that *S. babylonica* should be
grown in cemeteries because of its melancholy, poetic and
scriptural associations. He described its foliage as flowing 'like
the dishevelled hair and graceful drapery of a sculptured
mourner over a sepulchral urn'.

Other designers considered the willow's prime position was
by an ornamental lake, where the reflected light encouraged it to
stretch its twigs towards the water.

The Chinese discovered that compatibility long before the
weeping willow came to Europe. *S. babylonica* lines the lake by
the Summer Palace in Beijing, and the willow from Yu Yuan in
Shanghai was exported to the world on the willow pattern plate.

The Age, 28 October 1986, p. 32.

River red gum: a tree for nostalgia

Ask a homesick Aussie to picture a gum-tree and one of
many species may come to mind – the elegant lemon-
scented gum (*Eucalyptus citriodora*), the haunting ghost-gum (*E.
papuana*), the showy Western Australian flowering gum (*E.
ficifolia*) or the soaring mountain ash (*E. regnans*).

Odds are, however, that nostalgia will evoke the image of *E.
camaldulensis*, familiar companion to the river bank, thickset
guardian of the stock paddock or bystander along the highway.

Aborigines used the bark of *E. camaldulensis*, the river red
gum, for their canoes and they steeped their fishing lines in its
sap to prevent them fraying. European colonists created an

insipid blue or green ink by boiling the sap in an iron pot.

Bushmen kept an alert eye on the branches of this tree, sadly known as the 'widow-maker' because of its tendency to shed a bough without warning.

That reputation did not deter crowds from gathering under a river red gum in the Botanic Gardens, Melbourne, in 1850 to hear Victoria proclaimed a separate colony from New South Wales.

Three years earlier there had been a move to recognise the species as *E. rostrata*, a name widely accepted in Australia, but a quirk of history intervened.

As early as 1832 Friedrich Dehnhardt, the curator at the Camalduli gardens in Naples, described specimens of this eucalyptus growing there. Unfortunately no record of the origin of those trees has been found.

It could be that the seeds were distributed through London or Paris collectors, or even through a Spanish or Austrian connection as Naples was, at that time, subject to Hapsburg rule.

When the existence of an earlier name was realised, the Australian name, *E. rostrata*, had to give way to the older *E. camaldulensis* and recognition of the Neapolitan propagation.

As for the common name, gum-tree, we owe that to the English buccaneer, William Dampier. After an unexpected landfall on the coast of north-western Australia in 1688, he noted in his journal 'trees where the gum distils out of the knots or cracks'.

The Age, 6 December 1986, p. 22.

River red gum (*Eucalyptus camaldulensis*) located at St Kilda Junction, Melbourne in the 1980s. Illustrator: Anita Podwyszynski

Gentian and lobelia are the true blues

The color blue has powerful appeal. I know gardeners who are obsessive in their plantings of that color – hydrangeas, ceanothus, agapanthus, delphiniums, ageratum, forget-me-nots and hyacinths.

Propagation of the blue poppy, one of the most beautiful flowers in existence, fascinated gardeners throughout the world in the late 1920s. But for me, true blue in flowers is represented by gentian and lobelia.

Gentian (named for King Gentius of Illyria) recalls walking among the mountains of Switzerland, while lobelia, which I regarded initially as a prosaic bedding plant, assumed a magical quality after reading Patrick Synge's account of an expedition to the Mountains of the Moon.

Named after the Belgian Mathias de l'Obel, botanist to James I, the lobelia species – red as well as blue – were introduced into England from America in the 17th century.

One of the blue species, *Lobelia syphilitica*, received its unusual specific from Linnaeus, whose pupil Pehr Kalm reported that American Indians used it as a treatment for venereal disease.

Africa is the continent,

however, which produced the greatest variety of lobelia, ranging from the dainty *L. erinus* of the Cape of Good Hope to the gigantic species found on the mountains of Central Eastern Africa.

Vita Sackville-West 'put in a good word for lobelia' urging her readers to 'think of it in terms of the Mediterranean at its best' and advising them to plant *L. erinus* 'Cambridge Blue' in generous patches rather than as an edging.

In *Mountains of the Moon*, Patrick Synge describes the giant lobelias – the two-metre-tall stout obelisk spikes of deep blue flowers of *L. elgonensis*, the decoratively rich purplish blue flowers of *L. bequaertii* whose spikes thrust upward to three metres, and *L. wollastonii*.

Synge considered *L. wollastonii* (found in the heather zone of Mount Ruwenzori) 'the finest of all the lobelias when in flower ... a delicate shade of powder blue ... between the long woolly bracts which are densely covered with a greyish blue pubescence so that the whole spike, often 15 feet (4.5 metres) in height, is pale silvery blue in appearance'.

Imagine it in moonlight or decorated, as often happens, with snow and icicles!

The Age, 3 February 1987, p. 21.

In love with a love apple

One of summer's gardening pleasures is the tomato harvest. Picking the turgid fruit, the sun still radiant in its flesh, makes the midge and mosquito-ridden hours of watering finally worthwhile.

Tomatoes boast an ancestry dating back beyond the Aztec civilisation of Central America. The progenitor, *Lycopersicum cerasiforme*, can still be found in the wild in Peru; a reminder that the South American continent is a rich area for plant research by botanists, dietitians, pharmacists and conservationists.

The path to the gardens and greenhouses of 16th century Europe was a meandering one for the tomato. Spanish *conquistadores* brought back seeds with the Peruvian gold.

Popular belief is that a Spanish priest first grew the plant in his monastery garden. Then a visiting Moor admired the plant and took seeds back to Morocco. From there an Italian sailor took them to his homeland which bestowed the name *pomo de mori* (the Moorish apple) on the fruit.

Europe regarded the new import with considerable caution. The Italian botanist Matthiolus labelled it *mala insana* because it belonged to the family *Solanaceae*, notorious for deadly nightshade.

Acceptance was slow, although its reputation as an aphrodisiac encouraged the

French to call it the love apple – *pomme d'amour* – and gave it a social status that persisted for centuries.

By 1559, none less than Lord Burghley was growing tomatoes in England. They were produced, as Gerard was later to write, 'for interest or ornament or beauty of fruit'.

Centuries later, Flora Thompson in *Lark Rise to Candleford* reinforced the doubt country folk had towards tomatoes: 'Love-apples they be, though some hignorant folks be a callin' 'em tommy-toes ... nasty sour things they be, as only gentry can eat.'

Twentieth century commercial cultivation and cannery processing put paid to the old wives' tale that the red color of the fruit was nature's way of warning people that the plant was deadly.

You may debate whether *Lycopersicum esculentum* is a fruit or a vegetable. My Tiny Tims and Sweet Bites convince me it is a berry which places it in the fruit bowl – and very decoratively, too.

The Age, 10 March 1987, p. 28.

Adam's fall may be linked to his covering fig leaves

My friend Helen has offered more contenders for Eden's 'Tree of Knowledge' and she has taken me to task for neglecting Judaic commentaries in my account of the pomegranate.

She referred me to the 'Talmud' which claims the forbidden tree was a fig: 'By the very thing by which they [Adam and Eve] were disgraced, were they restored.'

The 'Midrash' explains this idea further. 'Adam tried to gather leaves from the tree to cover parts of their bodies but he heard one tree after another say 'This is the thief who deceived the Creator ... take no leaves from me'. Only the fig-tree allowed him to take its leaves because it was the forbidden fruit.'

Certainly the fig is mentioned in records of many early civilisations. Its value as a food was enhanced by its drying quality which made it easily stored and transported.

Four thousand years before the birth of Christ the Egyptians planted it. Phoenician traders probably introduced it to customers in Greece, India and perhaps even China. In ancient Greece, the fig had assumed sufficient importance for Herodotus to write about its cultivation.

To the Romans, too, it was

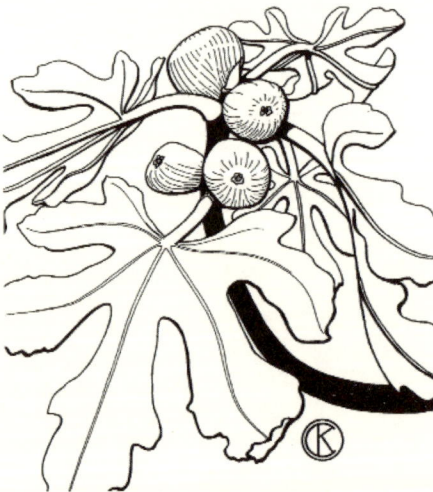

important – chiefly as slaves' food. A few patrician epicures recommended the Spanish figs which were semi-dried so that the natural shape and color were retained. On occasions, however, for those with malice and murder in mind, the fig was a convenient carrier of poison.

The fig was grown often in mediaeval monastic gardens and it featured in pictures adorning manuscripts. Early Christian painting and sculpture used the fig leaf to hide genitalia. Some scholars believe it was the palmate, or hand-like, shape of the fig leaf that occasioned this convention.

Further rabbinic opinion on the identity of the tree of knowledge includes wheat, grapes and the esrog or citron which reached Europe around 300 BC.

Theophrastus wrote about the citron, referring to it as the Persian or Medean apple. It was the Roman writer, Pliny, who first used the name citron. The related, and more modern, lemon had its place in mediaeval religious symbolism through an association with the Virgin Mary.

As a deliciously flavorsome fruit the fig might well present a tempting face to those who would be tempted, but the whole debate on the fruit of the 'Tree of Knowledge' simply highlights the challenge facing botanical or horticultural historians.

The Age, Tuesday 14 April 1987, p. 26.

Ivy has a proud heritage

How any self-respecting parent could ever label a daughter Ivy has always puzzled me. The poor girl must surely suffer wisecracks about 'a clinging vine' or being 'a climber'.

But the plant has a distinguished history. The Egyptian god, Osiris, benefactor of agricultural knowledge, wreathed his wand of authority in ivy.

Pliny the Elder, a mine of information on horticulture in classical times, claims Bacchus was the first to use ivy garlands and he quotes Theophrastus in relating how Alexander the Great's soldiers returning from India wore headbands of rare ivy.

Celebratory garlands of holly and ivy passed into Christmas tradition and featured in carols and wassailing.

'The sign of the bush', a festoon of ivy on a pole beside the door, meant that good cheer was to be had inside. Chaucer mentions the 'alestake' which inns began to use to advertise their trade and the quaint saying 'a good wine needs no bush' originated from this custom.

The great era of ivy lasted from about 1850 to 1920, beginning after the introduction into Britain of *Hedera colchica* from the Odessa Botanic Gardens in the 1840s.

Three decades later the Royal Horticultural Society had established an ivy collection at Chiswick and was testing 40 varieties. Shirley Hibberd's classic, *The Ivy*, published in 1872, guaranteed ivy a place in English gardens until the outbreak of the 1914 war.

Thereafter, Americans, impressed by England's creeper-clad ancient monuments, developed a taste for ivy on the walls of their colleges.

And so, dear ladies who bear the name, Ivy, yours is a proud and ancient heritage. I guess I would rather be an Ivy than a Thistle!

The Age, 5 May 1987, p. 28.

The Pasque flower*

Vita Sackville-West described the Pasque flower, *Pulsatilla vulgaris*, as

Lavender petals sheathed in silver floss,
Soft as the ruffle of a kitten's fur.

In folk-lore this flower predated Christianity in northern Europe. The bright green dye obtained from its petals was used to stain and decorate eggs – the spring symbols of fertility and new life.

Christian missionaries to Europe linked the flower, because of its flowering time, with the Paschal and Passover ceremonies. But pagan Nordic associations lingered in the suggestion that the herbal properties of *Pulsatilla* were more effective when taken by a flaxen-haired maiden with blue eyes, or the legend that the plant bloomed only where Saxon or Danish blood had fallen.

The Age, 2 June 1987, p. 27.
* title provided by HF

Pears have a rich heritage, by any name

The names given to varieties of fruit are a rich source of historical reference. Take pears. Although the cultivated pear probably arrived in Britain with the Romans, it was the mediaeval French varieties that held pride of place on court tables after the Norman invasion – 'Bergamotte', 'Beurre', and 'Bon Chretien'.

Crusaders setting out for the Holy Land favored the last-mentioned, particularly if they were produced in a monastic garden. Many varieties of old English pears also had names of ecclesiastical origin.

'Warden' pears, grown at Warden Abbey, were baked as a warm and spicy delicacy for sale on the feast of St Simon and St Jude in late October, and 'Martin' pears ripened at Martinmas.

The 17th century cavalier poet Sir John Suckling likened his love's cheek to a pear.

> For streaks of red were mingled there
> Such as are on a Catherine pear
> (The side that's next the sun).

His lines suggest a fruit honoring the memory of St Catherine and cultivated in espalier fashion.

The origin of the name 'Choke-pear' is less clear. Some authorities attribute the name to the astringent taste which shocks the palate causing the eater to cough; others relate the name to the story of Druscus, son of the Roman emperor Claudius, who choked to death on a pear.

In 1640, John Tradescant's garden boasted 49 pear varieties

because he strove 'to obtain all the rarest fruit he could hear of in … Christendom, Turkey, or the whole world'.

John Pea wrote of 20 pear varieties in his *Pomona* (1665) while Alexander Pope, a dedicated horticulturist as well as a notable writer, mentions in his correspondence the despatch of three grafts of choice pears, 'Chaumontelle', 'Vingouleuse' and 'Epine d'Hiver'.

While Captain Cook sailed towards the Pacific, a schoolmaster in Berkshire produced a new strain of the 'Bon Chretien' variety. It was sold by Richard Williams in his nursery near London and was taken to Massachusetts.

William Hooker illustrated this impressive pear in color in 1817 for the horticultural society's publication *Transactions*. It became known as the 'Williams' pear, while its American counterpart took the name 'Bartlett' after the owner of the property on which it grew.

Australia pays tribute to both England and America by calling the pear 'Williams' when it appears in the greengrocery and 'Bartlett' when it is canned. With 'Packham's Triumph' and 'Winter Cole', Australia has extended the choice of pear varieties.

Let the poet yearn for a 'blossomed pear-tree in the hedge' and let the lover wish a partridge in it: the gardener rejoices in the pear-tree's rich heritage.

The Age, 30 June 1987, p. 25.

The harbinger of spring is good enough to eat

L ilac time is a special moment in spring, as Ivor Novello recognised. In Melbourne, interest in Edwardian houses and gardens is bringing *Syringa vulgaris* back into favor.

Introduced into Europe from China by way of the Mughal gardens of Kashmir and Persia, lilac was mentioned in the description of the *giardino segreto* belonging to the Barberini family who lived in Siena in the 1630s.

It was also popular in England where John Worledge wrote of its 'branches of fine, white, scented flowers in April and May'. His contemporary, John Rea, promoted *S. persica* for its greater fragrance.

By the mid-17th century Adriaen van der Donck recorded the introduction of lilac to the Dutch settlement of Manhattan, and nearly a century later John Bartram described lilacs flowering in Williamsburg, Virginia.

The tubular form of the flower prompted Linnaeus to give lilac the generic name *Syringa*. However, another botanist chose the same name for mock orange (which Linnaeus had earlier dubbed *Philadelphus*). Popular confusion followed even though, according to the protocol of botanical nomenclature, the older Linnaean names had precedence.

Genus *Syringa* numbers about 30 species. Unusual members are *S. reflexa*, the nodding lilac from Central China, *S. amurensis*, the Amur River lilac, which has a large white inflorescence not unlike that of privet, *S. lanciniata*, which produces prinnate leaves in spring and entire leaves in summer, and the Hungarian lilac (*S. josikaea*) with its attractive foliage – dark green on the upper side and greyish green underneath.

Although cultivated in Europe for more than 300 years, *S. vulgaris* remained unnoticed by hybridisers until Victor Lemoine developed the French lilacs famed for their color, size and fragrance.

Vita Sackville-West favored the fragrant miniature *S. palibiniana*, a native of Korea, while in Victoria, Joan Law-Smith considers the perfume of the cultivar 'Vestale' the loveliest in her Macedon garden.

French writer Colette was of a different mind. Writing about the changing scent of lilac, she said: ' … it … has the distinct smell of scarab beetles until the moment of blossoming, frothing, white, mauve, blue, purple, when it fills the suburban trains, the Metro and the children's strollers with its toxic aroma of prussic acid.'

In spite of that tart judgment you will find specialist collections of lilac in Kew Gardens, London; in the Arnold Arboretum in Boston, Massachusetts; in Highland Park, Rochester, USA, and in the botanical gardens at Minsk in the USSR which Edward Hyams considered the finest lilac gardens in the world.

If you travel through the Peloponnese in April, you will notice that nearly every house has a lilac bush in the garden. Many of the Greek olive or citrus growers will tell you they use the lilac bush as a 'signal of spring'.

Next time you gather lilac, remember it is one of the world's most highly respected flowers. And if you think it looks good enough to eat, you are right. In France, lilac flowers are candied for export.

The Age, 27 October 1987, p. 35.

Language of flowers

Successively and successfully, pagan lore, Christian symbolism and commercial enterprise have gathered seasonal plants and bonded them into December traditions.

Holly, bright with berries, and resin-scented fir-trees epitomise Christmas celebrations in northern Europe and North America. But less familiar are the charming folk-tales linking plants with the Nativity.

Although in ancient Rome, holly (*Ilex aquifolium*) was a token of goodwill often sent as a gift during the festival of Saturn (17, 18 and 19 December), missionaries endowed it with Christian symbolism. The red berries were a reminder of Christ's redeeming blood, the white flowers stood for Mary's purity and its evergreen nature recalled eternal life. Well might the carollers sing, 'Of all the trees that are in the wood, the holly bears the crown'.

By Victorian times, sprigs of holly symbolised domestic happiness, friendship and good wishes. In the language of flowers, holly asked 'Am I forgotten?' and it decorated Christmas cards and Christmas crackers.

The tradition of the Christmas tree (usually *Picea abies*) originated in Germany. Prince Albert of Saxe-Coburg decked a spruce tree with stars, candles, tinsel and amusing baubles for his wife, Queen Victoria. Similar trees are now a focal point for family celebrations at Christmas.

Plants feature in many legends of the Nativity. One mediaeval story relates how Mary lay in the stable on a bed of *Galium verum* and *Pteridium aquilinum*. The ox and the ass ate the bracken leaving the softer, fragrant lady's bedstraw as a more appropriate mattress for the mother of Christ.

In Sicily, children put sprigs of penny-royal (*Mentha*

pulegium) into their beds on Christmas Eve to commemorate the belief that this low-growing member of the mint family first bloomed when Christ was born.

The poinsettia (*Euphorbia pulcherrima*) is known in Mexico as the *flor de la Noche-buscha*, or the flower of the Nativity. A local legend tells how a young girl wished to offer a gift at the Christmas Eve service. She picked a common euphorbia from the roadside and placed it on the altar in the brightly lit church. As she turned to go home, she noticed that the lights seemed to become brighter and brighter and that her flower was beginning to turn red.

Botanists and gardeners know that strong and constant overhead light causes the bracts of *Euphorbia pulcherrima* to turn bright red. Potted dwarf poinsettias offer the traditional Christmas colors of red and green in a decorative way.

Countries of the Southern Hemisphere are adding new flowers to the Christmas garland. The carefree, summer holidays

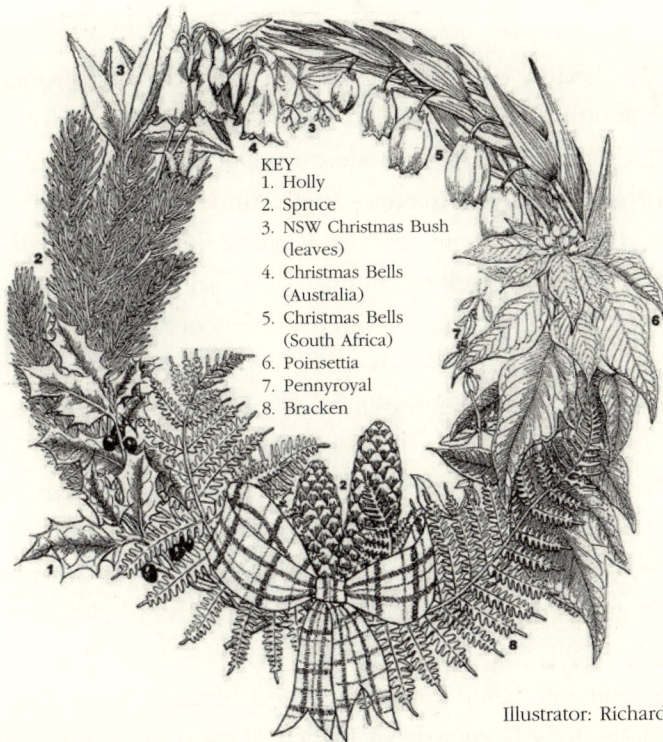

KEY
1. Holly
2. Spruce
3. NSW Christmas Bush (leaves)
4. Christmas Bells (Australia)
5. Christmas Bells (South Africa)
6. Poinsettia
7. Pennyroyal
8. Bracken

Illustrator: Richard Barley

of my childhood were memorable for seeking 'Black Prince' cicadas, discovering pockets of gaudy Christmas bells (*Blandfordia grandiflora*) and gathering bunches of New South Wales Christmas bush (*Ceratopetalum gummiferum*).

Doubtless children in other countries are fond of their local Christmas flowers – the bright, orange-red Christmas bells of South Africa (*Sandersonia aurantiaca*), the glowing Christmas jewels (*Aechmea racinae*) of South America, or the striking Mexican Christmas candles (*Tillandsia imperialis*).

The Age, 22 December 1987, p. 13.

*The protea**

Wracked by regrettable tension recalling Lincoln's America, South Africa may neglect research on its superlative botanical heritage to concentrate on political preoccupations. A land of great botanical interest, South Africa is symbolised by the protea. The name commemorates Proteus, the old man of the sea, who would foretell the future, it was said, if he was caught. Menelaus, king of Sparta, captured Proteus only to find him changing into incredible shapes to escape his captor.

The evanescent creature inspired Linnaeus to name a genus *Protea* and later Professor Jussieu gave the name *Proteaceae* to the plant family which includes the Australian natives *Banksia, Telopea, Grevillea, Stenocarpus, Dryandra* and *Hakea*.

Protea neriifolia was the first of the genus to be described and illustrated. In 1605 Clusius wrote of it as a graceful kind of thistle.

Seventeenth century exploration encouraged exotic plant collections. Kew Gardens sent Francis Masson to the Cape, and proteas were a significant feature of his collection.

Protea repens, popularly known as sugarbush, was used as the symbol of the Cape of Good Hope during the jubilee celebrations of the Kirstenbosch Botanic Gardens in 1963.

Thirteen years later the Government chose the King Protea (*P. cynaroides*) to replace the white arum lily (*Zantedeschia aethiopica*) as the official floral emblem of the Republic of South Africa.

Proteas are native only to Africa but they have migrated successfully to California, Israel, Provence, New Zealand and Australia.

The astonishing range of these flowers includes the showy *Protea magnifica,* the modest *P. nana,* the fringed protea (*P. laurifolia*), the peach protea (*P. grandiceps*), the nodding protea (*P. pendula*) and the snow protea (*P. cryophila*).

You can see a selection of the African members of the *Proteaceae* at the southern end of the Hopetoun Lawn in the Royal Botanic Gardens – *Protea compacta, P. cynaroides, Leucadendron argenteum, Leucospermum cordifolium* and *Serruria florida.*

The special plantings in these gardens all have South African flora in their midst. The woolly treasure flower (*Gazania rigens var. leucolaena*) and *Helichrysum retortum* flourish in the Grey Garden, *Pelargonium grossularioides* and *Santolina chamaecyparissus* add interest to the Herb Garden and many varieties of lithops and crassula provide interest in the arid display house.

The Age, 23 February 1988, p. 24.
* title provided by HF

A floral lesson of Christ's Passion

Many of us associate passionfruit with pavlova rather than with Passiontide, forgetting that more than 400 years ago resourceful missionaries in Brazil used a local flower to illustrate the story of the Crucifixion.

They taught that the white color of *Passiflora* was a symbol of purity and the bluish tint a symbol of Heaven. The outer petals represented the 10 faithful disciples. (Doubting Thomas and treacherous Iscariot were botanically ostracised, it seems.)

The five anthers stood for the five wounds; the leaf represented the spear; the tendrils, the whips; the three stigmas, the nails and the inner corona, the crown of thorns.

The three-day flowering period reminded the preachers of the three years of Christ's ministry, while the enthusiasm with which the indigenous population gorged on the fruit convinced the Jesuits that the local people were thirsting for Christianity.

The Age, 29 March 1988, p. 24.

Touch of Mexican sun

Among the various attractions of the famous English garden, Biddulph Grange, in its heyday was the dahlia walk. In fact, in the first half of the 19th century dahlia gardens were *de rigueur* throughout Europe.

Both England and France were indebted to Spain for these colorful flowers from Mexico, blooming now in Melbourne gardens. The dahlia had impressed the Spanish missionaries who sent tubers to the botanist Monardes at Seville and to Abbe Cavanilles at the Escorial gardens, near Madrid. The new import was named after a student of Linnaeus – Dr Anders Dahl.

The wife of the British ambassador to Spain, Lady Mary Holland, sent dahlia seeds home to England in 1804. These were more successful than the first dahlia flowers introduced into England in 1789 by the daughter-in-law of the third Earl of Bute.

James Veitch the Younger acclimatised and developed the dahlia for English conditions with such success that the Exeter Dahlia Show became famous and 19th century florists raised the classes of dahlia we know today: pompom, cactus, star.

The French ambassador

to Mexico sent dahlias (the Mexican cocoxochitl) back to France in mistake for the cochineal beetle. The plants were nurtured in the Jardin des Plantes in the hope that their tubers might provide a substitute for the potato.

However, the Empress Josephine fell in love with the dahlia flower and she planted dahlias at Malmaison. Then an ambitious lady-in-waiting asked for a single dahlia from the garden.

Denied the favor, the scheming woman encouraged her lover to bribe a gardener to steal 100 dahlia plants.

The plot was discovered. The lady-in-waiting was dismissed and her lover banished from court. The gardener was fired and in fury Josephine ordered all her dahlia beds to be dug up forever.

Bright as the Mexican sun, the exotic dahlia suited the flamboyant garden of Biddulph Grange, at Staffordshire. Unfortunately this garden has declined and decayed to an alarming degree. Efforts are being made to restore and preserve it but lack of finance is jeopardising the program and a public appeal has been launched.

The Age, 3 May 1988, p. 27.

Symbol of love and fertility

A piquant, palate-cleansing sauce served with chicken at a lunch some weeks ago revived my interest in the quince, for that was what flavored the memorable dish.

Offered a quince today, few people would eat it raw. Yet that was how it was enjoyed in antiquity when palates were not conditioned by sugar to spurn sharp tastes.

A member of the rose family, *Cydonia oblongata* has been cultivated for more than 4000 years, spreading far from its native habitat of Anatolia and Persia.

Ancient civilisations set great store by the quince. Classical Greek trade records indicate that Athens imported the fruit from Corinth, the bountiful region better known for its currant grapes. Crete, too, was renowned for fine varieties of quince.

By Roman times fashions in food were changing and Pliny considered that the Mulvian quince was the only one suitable for eating raw.

According to Petronius, quinces were useful table decorations. He describes how, studded with thorns, they looked like sea-urchins at the fabled feast of Trimalchio.

The 'golden apple' of the Hesperides is sometimes thought to have been a quince although other contenders for this honor are the orange and the lemon.

Dedicated to Venus, the quince was a symbol of love, fertility and happiness. Eating it was part of wedding ritual, and well-wishers tossed quinces into the bridal chariot for a fruitful future.

In mediaeval Europe the status of the quince remained high. Chaucer refers to the fruit as 'coines', suggesting a strong influence from France where the word for quince is *coing*.

Orleans was famous for its *cotignac*, a quince conserve, and when Joan of Arc arrived to lift the siege of the town she was proudly offered the local product.

Italy, too, had its special quince marmalade known as *cotognati*, and the Portuguese made their quinces into *marmelo* which some people claim was the origin of the word marmalade.

Much later, the Massachusetts Bay colony requested quince seeds from England and there are reports of well-established quince trees in Virginia by 1720.

In interior areas of South Africa, colonists found the quince a far hardier fruit-producer than the apple.

Today the ubiquitous food market chains with their dominant canning interests rarely put quinces into our supermarket trolleys. This is very different from the village economy where the hedgerows freely offered nuts, berries and fruits like quinces to all who passed by with a basket on their arm.

The Age, 31 May 1988, p. 31.

Sweet corn stands tail

It is hardly grass for the urban plot but it looks good in the country vegetable garden. I like it as a symbol of nature's bounty towards man. *Zea mays*, or sweet corn, grows so confidently, thrusting itself sunwards tall and leafy. Was ever a more generous harvest packaged so beautifully in floss and pale green wrapper?

I relish the joy of house-guests from the city invited to pick their supper. The cob snaps crisply from the stalk, then there is the rustle of corn-shucking and finally the plop into boiling water. After the ritual anointing with butter and pepper we become the latest in a line of corn-eaters stretching back to the Incas, the Aztecs and the Mayas.

Corn and memories ... of polenta in Italy, hoe-cakes in Nebraska, popcorn at Coney Island, tortillas in Mexico and mealies in Transvaal. Snatches of popular songs '... as corny as Kansas in August' and corn 'as high as an elephant's eye' in 'Oklahoma'.

The beauty of corn does not fade. Three cobs have graced my kitchen for years – one of burnished brown kernels, another of copper color and the third an assortment of cream, rose, purple and black. The silk has dried but the shucks remain bleached and paper-like.

The pleasure garden welcomes the dwarf ornamental cultivars (and these are suitable for the city garden) – the smart yellow, green, white and pink striped leaves of *Z. mays* 'Japonica quadricolor', or the sinuous leaves of *Z. mays* 'Gracillima variegata'.

Sweet corn also brings recollections of the enthusiasm of the late Dame Margaret Blackwood at Melbourne University who came to love *Zea mays* through her research and studies as a botanist and geneticist.

This popular plant appeals to all the senses. It sustains body, mind and spirit whether you are gardener, cook, traveller, artist or scientist. The formidable Harriet Martineau commented during her American travels: 'A man who has corn may have everything.'

The Age, 21 June 1988, p. 23.

Acacia Avenue, and no wattles in sight

In spite of its name, I find Acacia Avenue the most pleasing of the spring vistas which focus on the pagoda in London's Kew Gardens.

Any self-respecting Australian would expect wattles in Acacia Avenue. Not so, for the trees that frame the view are *Robinia pseudoacacia* (the black locust or false acacia) and *Gleditsia triacanthos* (the honey locust).

Were ever trees saddled with such unfortunate common names? False Acacia Avenue (spiv-like), Black Locust Avenue (plaguey) and Honey Locust Avenue (cloying) are most inappropriate addresses for an elegant pagoda!

The association of these trees, native to North America, with locusts appears to have arisen from the perceived likeness of their seed-pods to the insect on which the Bible claims John the Baptist fed. Scholarly disputation produced another view: that John ate the fruit of the carob tree (*Ceratonia siliqua*), which also bears locust-like seed pods.

The black locust was one of the first American trees sent to Europe and by about 1600 Jean Robin, herbalist to Henri IV, was growing it in Paris. His name is remembered in the tree's generic label. In the wine-producing districts of France, you may notice stands of robinias from which the vine stakes will be cut. Vignerons value the long-lasting quality of the wood.

Impressed by such usefulness, the English journalist William Cobbett came home from America in 1823 to promote the black locust tree. He had an interest in a plant nursery on Long Island which raised seeds for the English market, but the business collapsed when the resulting trees grew crooked and branched too soon.

With such far-flung associations, only the use of botanical names saved the locust trees from an identity crisis. Besides, you could not find prettier names than *Robinia* and *Gleditsia* for such graceful trees. Acacia Avenue indeed!

The Age, 30 August 1988, p. 30.

Sequoyah – the man and the tree

Readers of *The Times* in 1853 pondered over photographs showing a stand of newly discovered trees in California. Their great size generated correspondence in the paper for a fortnight, and the main interest was on an appropriate name for the gigantic plants.

Professor Lindsay, wanting to commemorate England's brilliant general, advocated *Wellingtonia gigantea*. Americans favored their military hero, and suggested *Washingtonia gigantea*.

Before compatriots could offer *Napoleonia gigantea*, a knowledgeable and diplomatic Frenchman argued for *Sequoia gigantea*. The botanist Decaisne's nomination recognised characteristics which the giant tree shared with the Californian redwood (*Sequoia sempervirens*), and the name was accepted.

The brouhaha surrounding the discovery of that first grove of giant redwoods in the notorious Calaveras County of gold-fevered California strikes a contrast with the lack of publicity accorded the achievements of Sequoyah, after whom the trees were named.

When miner-cum-backwoodsman Downes, who discovered the trees while trailing a grizzly bear, returned to base boasting of his find, the laconic Californian pioneers treated the account as just another tall story of the frontier. Only by inventing a story of a comparably gigantic bear was A. T. Downes able to goad his companions into seeking the trees.

Once the trees were seen, however, news of the discovery raced through the lumber camps of the Sierra Nevada and the axemen set to work.

Unlike the lumbermen, the American Indians did not threaten the forests. Their wants were few. Dead sticks sufficed to feed their fires. They burnt the prairie grasses only to control the natural debris which could fuel a rogue fire and pose a serious danger to the trees.

Sequoyah was a remarkable Indian. The son of a Cherokee woman and a German colonist, he faced the thrusts of very different cultures. As Cherokee genealogy emphasises the maternal line, Sequoyah's link with his mother's race was strong but he could also see the strengths of his father's way of life.

Born in Tennessee in 1770, Sequoyah followed the customary pursuits of the American backwoodsman –

hunting and fur-trading. He was curious about the ways of the Europeans and he acquired silver-smithing skills.

Although he knew no English, he observed a strange custom among his father's people – the use of 'talking leaves'. He saw men look at a piece of paper and he noticed that symbols on it spoke to them.

Sequoyah determined to represent Cherokee words by animal figures and symbols, but this scheme was too cumbersome. The inventive Indian then worked on a means of representing syllables. For 12 years he labored with pin on stone, with knife on wood, with charred stick on bark and with pen on paper.

In 1821, he finally convinced people that his syllabary was a practical means of communicating. When people spoke to Sequoyah's children out of their father's hearing, the children wrote the message and Sequoyah was able to read the very words spoken.

His tribe appointed him envoy to Washington, DC, in the fruitless attempt to secure a more just solution in the matter of Indian tribal lands.

There after, Sequoyah taught thousands of Cherokees to read and write – even when he was part of the forced migration to Oklahoma. All along that 'Trail of Tears' Sequoyah labored with his writing. He wrote a tribal constitution, a Cherokee version of the Old Testament and he published a weekly paper in Cherokee.

A statue of Sequoyah stands in the Capitol in Washington. But how much more appropriate that the world's largest living thing (trees are sometimes bigger than whales or elephants) should bear the name of that peaceful and great-hearted man.

The Age, 13 December 1988, p. 30.

Australia's beloved warrior

Fashions in colors change as much as fashions in food or flowers. In Sydney Town Hall the windows commemorating Australia's Centenary glowed red and blue, and featured waratah (*Telopea speciosissima*) and flannel flowers (*Actinotus helianthus*) as decorative borders. Not a sprig of wattle anywhere and no hint of the vibrant yellow and green that characterised Australia's Bicentenary celebrations.

From the designs of Lucien Henry in the 1880s to the prints of Margaret Preston in the 1930s, the waratah was a dominant decorative motif symbolising an Australia represented essentially by New South Wales.

Dr John White, surgeon-general with the First Fleet, sent a dried waratah back to the Linnaean Society in London. Later, the president of the Royal Society identified it as *Embothrium speciosissimum*, suggesting some likeness to the Chilean firebush. (Much later the Australian tree waratahs were placed in the genus *Oreocallis*, which has species native to Peru and Ecuador; evidence supporting the Gondwanaland link with the South American continent.)

It was R. Brown who named the waratah in its own right, choosing the appropriate generic *Telopea* – seen at a distance. Lacking botanical knowledge, early colonists called the flower the tulip tree of New South Wales. To the Aborigines, it was waratah and they had many stories about it.

Krubi, a maiden of the Burragorang tribe, made herself a red cloak of rock wallaby skin and the crest feathers of the gang-gang cockatoo. Enamored of a young hunter, she awaited his return each day standing on the ridge that protected the valley.

One day her warrior did not return. Krubi remained at her

vantage point while her tears watered the native flowers. Her tribe moved on leaving her to her grief.

On the spot where she died there bloomed a flower whose stalk was as upright as Krubi's beloved warrior, its leaves pointed like his spear and its flowers the flaming color of her magnificent cloak.

The other species of Telopea – *T. mongaensis* (Braidwood waratah), *T. truncata* (Tasmanian waratah) and *T. oreades* (Gippsland tree waratah) – are less well known.

Although *T. speciosissima* is exported commercially, it is not a contender for the title of Australia's national flower. Unlike the wattle, its habitat is limited to eastern Australia and it is the state flower of New South Wales.

The waratah is enjoying renewed interest as a subject for the home garden, and as a cut flower, and the work of the Australian National Botanic Gardens has made Canberra a centre for new cultivars.

A recent publication *The Waratah*, by Paul Nixon (Kangaroo Press), is a timely reminder of the plant's place in Australia's history and culture.

The Age, 7 February 1989, p. 25.

A lucky bouquet fit for a king

Few who stay in the hotel at Saint-Paul-Trois-Châteaux between Montelimar and Orange in the Rhône Valley realise that this is where the charming French tradition of offering lily-of-the valley on the first of May originated.

In 1560 the young King Charles IX and his mother, Catherine of Medici, were travelling through that area. The chevalier Louis de Girard picked a bouquet of lily-of-the-valley from his château garden and presented it to the 10-year-old king for good luck.

The following year, on May Day, the king in his turn offered lily-of-the-valley to the ladies at court, wishing them luck and bidding them to continue the tradition in future.

The flower brought little fortune to poor Charles who later sanctioned the infamous massacre of St Bartholomew's Eve and subsequently died at the age of 28. The Chevalier de Girard was scarcely more fortunate – his family home is now a hotel and the lily-of-the-valley has long since disappeared from his garden.

After the French Revolution the royalist tradition of giving lily-of-the-valley vanished, to be revived in a different way this century when Paris couturiers gave the flower to their clients and their seamstresses on the first of May.

The city of Paris supported and extended the idea by allowing the sale of lily-of-the-valley in the streets without a permit – provided the seller

remained standing!

Convallaria majalis (or *muguet de bois* to the French) was known as 'mugget' in some areas of England, suggesting that, somewhere, sometime, the French word crossed the Channel. Perhaps St Leonard was a Norman knight.

In Sussex he is notable as a dragon-killer, and around the forest that bears his name, local folk-lore recounts how a fragrant white flower sprang from his blood when one of his more formidable dragon adversaries wounded him.

If St Leonard was responsible for the introduction of *C. majalis* into England, the French do not appear to acknowledge the fact.

The Age, 16 May 1989, p. 32.

Birth of the red, white and blue

This Friday, the French will celebrate their national day with Bicentennial ardor. Books and souvenirs marking the occasion have appeared in unending supply – flamboyant, opportunist or esoteric.

In the last category I find *Fleurs, Fêtes et Saisons* by Jean-Marie Pelt a pleasurable offering. The professor of pharmacology and vegetable biology at the University of Metz, and president of the European Ecological Institute, Pelt has considerable knowledge of plantlore, history and humanity.

A wonderful raconteur, he is capable of disarmingly imaginative logic in any case he puts – none more than his chapter on 'A Bunch of Flowers and the Flag', which is a Bicentennial whimsy.

Pelt takes the colors of the French flag – white, blue and red – and associates them with flowers of those colors in

French history.

White has been the color of France from time immemorial. It is associated with the fleur-de-lys, symbol of French royalty. The origin of the fleur-de-lys was not a white lily, but the yellow iris (*Iris pseudacorus*) which, it is said, showed Clovis a ford across the river Vienne and consequently gave him victory over the Visigoths in 507.

Thereafter Clovis adopted the iris for his standard and his successors maintained the custom. The lily/iris debate continues and sophists explain the white color of the fleur-de-lys by the fact that Iris was the Greek goddess of the rainbow whose colors combine to give white (or light)!

On 13 July 1789, the French revolutionary forces created a Parisian militia whose emblem was a blue and red cockade: red and blue were the colors of Paris. Three days after the fall of the Bastille, Louis XVI received the cockade to which he added white, the color of the king, in the vain hope that there would be an alliance between the king and the people of Paris.

During World War II, occupied France kept the national spirit alive each 14 July by making posies of red, white and blue field flowers: the tricolor flag could not be raised.

White was provided by the marguerite daisy which, Pelt is swift to emphasise, is the prototype of a socialist flower since it is a republic – botanically speaking – of many individual flowers!

The cornflower gave blue, the color of the revolutionary army uniform; although it can also be said that the 'champ d'azur' was the background

color for the armorial devises of the French kings.

The corn poppy provided the red. The seeds of this flower have an amazing ability to remain long in the ground without deteriorating. When soil is turned and the seeds are subjected to air and light, germination occurs. That is the explanation of the growth of many poppies in Flanders fields after the tremendous upheaval of earth in trench warfare, or the burgeoning of poppies at Thionville in 1977 when the gigantic Parisian ring-road was being constructed.

As common field-flowers, daisy, cornflower and corn poppy are victims of the destructive forces of man and machine. In their flowering they are as ephemeral as revolutions and in their seeds they are as long-lasting as revolutionary ideas. They are ideal floral symbols of the French Revolution.

The Age, 11 July 1989, p. 25.

A shrub to refresh man's weariness

Buddhist legend attributes the origin of *Camellia sinensis* to the penance of the holy man, Bodhidarma, who fell asleep during meditation. Haunted by carnal love, Bodhidarma cut off his eyelids to escape his spiritual anguish and remain awake forever.

Buddha was greatly moved by this sacrifice and he caused the holy man to sink into a deeper sleep. When Bodhidarma awoke he found his eyelids had been restored and a shrub with dainty eyelid-shaped leaves and snowy buds was growing beside him. He sensed the plant had a special quality affirming 'for all time to come men who drink of your sap shall find such refreshment that weariness shall never overcome them'. A delightful story of how the tea-bush was created.

Introduced to England in the mid-17th century, tea became a fashionable beverage commended in literature and art. The 18th century marked the beginning of interest in the camellia as a plant. Some authorities believe *C. japonica* arrived in London as a substitute for *C. sinensis*, which the East India Company had hoped to propagate and so avoid the tax on imported tea.

Dried specimens of *C. japonica* were received by London apothecary James Petiver in the late 17th century and in 1712 Engelbert Kaempfer, who had worked as a physician with the Dutch East India Company, included illustrations of *C. sinensis*, *C. japonica* and *C. sasanqua* in his *Amoenitatum Exoticarum*.

Working from Kaempfer's specimens, Linnaeus selected the name Camellia for the new genus as a tribute to the Jesuit missionary and botanist George Josef Kamel (latinised name, Camellus), who had collected plants in the Philippines.

The camellia had long been a favorite with Chinese mandarins and the first *C. japonica* to flower in England did so in about 1739 in the glasshouse of the remarkable amateur botanist Lord Petre of Thorndon Hall, Essex. At the same time André Michaux introduced it into America.

New varieties arrived in Europe from the Far East in rapid succession during the 19th century: *C. oleifera* (1811), *C. maliflora* (1818), *C. reticulata* (1820), *C. kissii* and *C. sasanqua* (1829), *C. rosaflora* (1858) and *C. hongkongensis* (1874).

European society adored the camellia. The consumptive Marguerite Gautier, who could not tolerate scented flowers,

adopted them as her hallmark and Dumas celebrated her as 'La Dame aux Camélias'; Paul Rivet mourned the loss of his beloved camellia garden destroyed in the Franco-Prussian war; Disraelian ladies wore camellias in their bonnets and their hair; Queen Victoria mentioned the red camellias at Osborne in her correspondence; the Duke of Sutherland cultivated an avenue of camellias under glass at his palace in the Midlands.

This obsession with camellias coincided with the pastoral settlement of Australia and the Macarthurs of Camden Park raised camellias as successfully as they did merinos.

In 1831 William Macarthur recorded the receipt of *C. japonica, C. wellbankiana, C. carnea, C. anemoniflora* and *C. myrtifolia*. By 1845 he could write '… we have raised four or five hundred seedlings' to which he had given 69 cultivar names. He issued catalogues regularly and dispatched plants to nurserymen and to enthusiastic amateur gardeners.

Of Macarthur's cultivars, 'Aspasia' (1850) and 'Cassandra' (1850) can be seen in the camellia bed in the Royal Botanic Gardens, Melbourne. There, too, are found other cultivars developed in Australia – T. W. Shepherd's 'Leviathan' and 'Speciosissima' and Silas Sheather's 'Sheatheri' and 'Henri Favre'.

Many dedicated camellians have been Australian, notably the late Professor E. G. Waterhouse whose garden is now a National Trust property. His name has been given to the National Camellia Garden at Caringbah, south of Sydney. There you can see the rare *C. higo* and hundreds of other distinctive varieties.

The Age, 18 July 1989, p. 22.

Spring brings magic of daffodil days

Certain days in early spring have a crystal quality born of sharp showers, stiff breezes and snatches of brilliant sunshine. For me, these are 'daffodil days'.

The narcissus family has exerted its spring magic down the ages. The generic name recalls the Greek youth who spurned the nymph Echo, and thereafter was condemned by the gods to admire his own image in a pool.

France has kept the classical name (*narcisse*) in common parlance whereas the English common name (daffodil) comes from a less romantic Greek source – asphodel.

In mythology, asphodel was a plant peculiar to the dead, one which the Egyptians left in their tombs. The earthly genus Asphodelus is quite unlike the narcissus family, as English botanist William Turner remarked in his *Herbal*:

> *I could never se thys herbe asphodelus – (affodyl) in*
> *England but ones for the herbe that the people calleth*
> *here affodil or daffodil is a kind of narcissus.*

Daffodilly or daffodowndilly enjoys a welcome place everywhere as the harbinger of spring. Daffodils decorate English churches at Easter. Together with the yew they are symbols of the resurrection and new life. Sometimes spring is early and Easter is late so the daffodils appear in Lent. Hence they have yet another popular name – Lenten lilies or Lents (quite as ugly a name as daffs).

Daffodils were mentioned in the earliest known English treatise on gardening, that of Mayster Ion the Gardener, written around 1400. Nearly 150 years later, William Turner recognised 24 species when writing his 'A Few Narcisse of Diverse Sortes' and his contemporary, Thomas Tusser, listed the daffodil as a strewing herb.

Thereafter daffodils disappear from the cottage flower lists to reappear with enhanced reputation in Sir Thomas Hanmer's *Garden Book* (1659), which recommended daffodils as a subject for 'four little bordered knots in the midst of a bordered knot'.

Neither had the bright daffodil escaped the poet's eye. Herrick and Shakespeare each praised the flower long before Wordsworth's 'heart with pleasure filled'.

The Lakes poet recorded the renewed interest in the narcissus family, underscoring the work of 19th century enthusiasts such as Covent Garden nurseryman Peter Barr, Edward Leeds or banker William Backhouse.

Barr was the instigator of the first Daffodil Conference in 1884. Breeding experiments by the Reverend George Engleheart produced 'Will Scarlett', exhibited in the first British Daffodil Show held in the Birmingham Botanical Gardens in April 1893 when three bulbs sold for £100.

An exhibitor in the early shows faced quite a daunting task. In 1898, a class one collection required from 100 to 600 blooms. By 1913, revised rules had reduced this number to 144.

Today the most demanding class at the Royal Horticultural Society show is the Bowles Cup – a total of 45 blooms. The secretary of the British Daffodil Society, Don Barnes, attributes the demise of huge exhibits to 'the changing social fabric and the new approach to gardening'.

Although potted 'Erlicheer' or a patch of 'April Love' in a private garden may give personal pleasure, the

breathtaking joy of daffodils belongs to public places.

The golden swathe bordering the Broad Walk in London's Hyde Park, the sweep of Pheasant's Eye (*Narcissus poeticus*) in the alpine meadows at Les Avants above Montreux, and the tazettas that carpet Pelopponesian glades are at the heart of a European spring.

Nor are we denied such pleasure. The daffodil paddock at St Erth, Blackwood, the slopes of Langley Vale, near Kyneton, and the Oak Lawn in the Royal Botanic Gardens are places of pilgrimage in the antipodean spring.

The Age, 19 September 1989, p. 24.

Origin of the species is under a cloud

Fact and fiction can become blurred in splendidly romantic stories about the arrival of exotic flowers in England. That darling of the Victorian era, the fuchsia, is a case in point.

One version of the fuchsia story relates how a nurseryman of Hammersmith, James Lee, noticed an exotic flower blooming on the windowsill of a humble dockland cottage in Wapping.

He found that the owner's son, a sailor, had brought the plant back from Santo Domingo. After hard bargaining, Lee eventually bought the plant for eight guineas and the promise of a rooted cutting. He subsequently raised 300 cuttings that sold for one guinea apiece.

The curator of the Liverpool Botanic Gardens, Mr Shepherd, wrote this story for the *Lincoln Herald* of 4 November 1831. But since Lee had died 36 years earlier, there was a curious time-lag in the telling.

According to John Loudon, however, a Captain Firth brought

two fuchsia plants back to the Royal Botanic Gardens, Kew, from South America in 1788. Soon after, Lee obtained a plant and found it easy to propagate many hundreds of cuttings; shrewdly controlling the sale of plants, he maintained the high price of one guinea for each.

The latter, more prosaic, story is more credible in its chronology. Margaret Meen in *Exotic Plants from the Royal Gardens Kew*, published in 1790, includes an illustration of *Fuchsia magellanica*. Meen came to London in the 1770s and exhibited at the Royal Academy from 1775 to 1785, that is, during Lee's working life.

The French priest and botanist Charles Plumier, who had named the genus after Leonard Fuchs, the 16th century German herbalist, had located it in Santo Domingo in 1703.

Whichever way the fuchsia arrived in England and Europe, nurserymen from England, Holland, France and Germany eagerly developed cultivars and 19th century colonists welcomed them. France produced the classic fuchsia 'Phenomenal', a large double scarlet and indigo bloom, and this was grown by William Guilfoyle in the Melbourne Botanic Gardens. A 'sport' from this plant was selected and named 'Countess of Hopetoun' after the wife of Australia's first Governor-General.

Botanical history is full of missing evidence. There is indeed a place for the popular story, and there is another place for the account of the professional introduction of new species. The thing is to know which is which. In the story of the fuchsia we seem to have a hybrid.

The Age, 19 December 1989, p. 22.

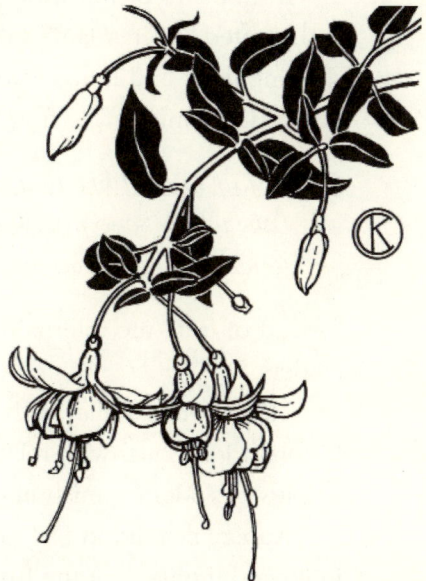

Aubergine – the Turks' gourmet delight

My sister Eleanor tends a well-established garden with friable soil, a well-drained slope, reticulated water supply and permanent settlement. She sympathised with my situation: land recently cleared of swamp paperbark (*Melaleuca squarrosa*), incipient bracken, poor drainage, heavy soil, tank water and intermittent settlement.

Knowledgeable on horticultural matters, Eleanor offered me selected seedlings that could endure the unpromising habitat. Confidently she assured me they would thrive on neglect. The flowers did – *Erigeron* and *Crowea exalata*. I held great expectations of her choice as a vegetable – the aubergine or eggplant (*Solanum melongena*) – despite its diabolic history.

In Book 10 of *Paradise Lost*, Milton described the vegetable I had planted. After Adam's fall, Satan and his host 'parcht with scalding thirst and hunger fierce' were themselves tempted by a luscious-looking purple fruit:

> *... fair to sight like that which grew Near that bituminous Lake where Sodom flamed. This was delusive, not the touch, but taste Deceived ...*

Instead of fruit, the infernal horde chewed bitter ashes, soot and cinders.

Milton was familiar with the story given by the Jewish historian Josephus, who related how he had seen the beautiful 'apples of Sodom' vanish into smoke when they touched the lips.

Aubergines did in fact grow near Sodom, where an insect infiltrated the flesh of the fruit causing it to decay into a powder without affecting the tempting external appearance.

Middle Eastern farmers protected the plant against the insect pest by putting pitch around the lower stem parts of the plant.

Small wonder the English preferred to grow *Solanum melongena* as an ornamental curiosity. It was the pukka sahibs of the Empire and their more daring memsahibs who ate the aubergine as brinjal – a fruit popular in India for centuries.

The earliest references to the aubergine are found in Chinese writings of the fifth century BC. The Chinese revere the aubergine for its antiquity and today tourists to China can purchase delightful carved figures of children holding an aubergine, a talisman for long life.

As Greek and Roman writers fail to mention the aubergine, it is likely that the Moors and Portuguese traders first introduced it to Europe. The Turks appreciated it as a gourmet delight. Their dish 'Fainting Priest' (aubergine stuffed with pine-nuts) was so delicious that a priest swooned with pleasure on sampling the heavenly combination.

Perhaps the popularity of the aubergine with the infidel Turks prejudiced Christians toward it. Perhaps its unpopularity was simply due to its membership of that fascinating family Solanaceae. The black sheep of the family – *Nicotiana* (tobacco), *Atropha belladonna* (deadly nightshade) and *Datura stramonium* (thornapple) sully the reputation of the more useful members – capsicums, paprika, tomatoes, potatoes and aubergines.

As for my egg-plants, they were obviously touched by Lucifer. They shrivelled and failed utterly to exhibit the virtues bestowed on them by my sister.

The Age, 5 June 1990, p. 24.

Summer Snow

Hot it may be, but Christmas in Australia has been a snowy,
showy celebration since colonial times, writes ALISON DALRYMPLE.

Before the days of tinsel, glitter and plastic, early Australian
settlers looked to the native flora for Christmas decoration.

In the backblocks of Maryborough in Queensland, E. S.
Sorenson explained how, at Christmas 'one of the principal
features is the gay array of bushes that deck the verandah posts
of the houses ... even the selector's hut, standing alone in a
wilderness of trees, is annually decorated this way.'

Particularly popular were plants evoking memories of snowy
English Christmases. *Melaleuca linariifolia*, often used as a street
tree in Melbourne clearly deserves its popular name of Snow in
Summer, and the falling petals of the early summer-flowering
Leptospermum species drift like snowflakes on the summer
breeze. The cultivar 'Pacific Beauty' offers a veritable snowstorm.

The Victorian Christmas bush (*Prostanthera lasianthos*) is an
elegant, aromatic shrub bearing white flowers smudged with
mauve. Like most of the mint bush family, it prefers the cool
protection of gullies and is more commonly found in the bush
than in horticulture.

The historian Geoffrey Blainey says women probably did
more than men to marry Christmas to this new land. He claims
the colonial women 'plucked any white flowering and called it,
nostalgically, the Christmas Bush. In their enthusiasm, they
almost made the snow appear before the eyes of children who
had never seen snow.'

Ceratopetalum gummiferum, the New South Wales Christmas
bush, is a striking summer beauty appearing increasingly in
suburban gardens. Its tiny creamy flowers spread a delicate lacy

shawl over the tree, and after they fade the pink sepals remain giving a distinctive rosy flush. A fairly slow-growing species in Victoria, it is often set back by frost. Cultivars include 'Christmas Snow' and 'White Christmas'.

Red and gold are other colors favored for festive occasions. On summer picnics in the Sutherland and Engadine areas south of Sydney, children would seek graceful Christmas bells (*Blandfordia grandiflora*). Happily, seed is now available to grow these in containers or in a moist, well-drained, sunny position in the garden.

The most spectacular and sweet-scented of the native Christmas plants is the Western Australian Christmas tree (*Nuytsia floribunda*). Its golden, almost orange shock of flowers brightens the sand plains around Perth from November to January. Up to 10 metres tall, it is claimed to be the largest parasitic plant in the world and needs the roots of a neighboring tree as host. Since first collected, it has proved notoriously difficult to cultivate, and remains so.

The botanical name recalls the Dutch navigator Pieter Nuyts, who explored the Western Australian coast and noted the species. The plant is associated also with the early plant gatherer Georgiana Molloy. Her bushwalks in the 1820s and '30s with her infant children uncovered a wealth of unknown plants, whose seed and seedlings she packaged immaculately and sent to avid botanists and gardeners in England. *Nuytsia* was particularly prized. She wrote in 1842, just before her death: 'I have been four times out in quest of *Nuytsia* and send you the small, small harvest. They are very difficult to obtain if not there the very day they ripen.'

Some gardeners like to commemorate particular occasions with a planting. Should you wish to record your first Christmas in a new

home, you might consider *Metrosideros tomentosa*, the New Zealand Christmas tree, or Pohutukawa. Tough, tolerating wind, salt or smog, its glossy leaves with a grey underside set off the brilliant red flowers. Clearly no reminder of a snowy European yuletide, it is more appropriate as a good gathering place for the Christmas barbecue or a convivial beer.

The Age, 23 December 1995, Extra, p. 10.

Spinach

Surprisingly Louis XIV and Popeye have something in common – a love of spinach.

Spinacea oleracea descended from the wild Persian spinach (*S. tetranda*) which travelled eastwards via Nepal to China where it was known as 'the Persian herb', and westwards with the Moors to eleventh century Avicenna.

By 1351 spinach had appeared in a list of vegetables recommended for monks on fast days. In the same century an anonymous 'menager de Paris' reported 'there is a species of chard called espinoche which is eaten at the beginning of Lent'.

Catherine of Medici was so fond of spinach that the phrase 'a la florentine' on a menu indicates the dish contains spinach. The word Viroflay is used for the same purpose because it was the area near Paris renowned for the cultivation of spinach.

La Quintinie, the court gardener at Versailles, planted spinach and a jesting ditty of the period tells how Louis XIV relished the vegetable although his doctor forbade it. Naturally Louis sent his courtiers to procure it shouting 'What, I am king of France and I cannot eat spinach!'

By the eighteenth century spinach was growing in the

American colonies and the meticulous Thomas Jefferson recorded three varieties in his garden notes.

There is great variety in modern cultivars. The American public, and presumably Popeye, prefer the curly leafed strain such as 'Bloomsdale' whereas Europeans favour the smooth leafed varieties.

Australian taste has supported *Chenopodium auricomum* or silver beet as a leaf vegetable. Indeed overseas this is sometimes known as Australian spinach.

There are few countries which do not have a vegetable popularly known as spinach. The botanical names however, show the difference.

Of historical interest is New Zealand spinach (*Tetragonia tetragonoides*) which grows wild in Japan, Australia and New Zealand. Captain Cook and his company ate it on their south sea voyage. Cook's log for May 6, 1770 records how the crew had dined on sting-ray and 'with it a dish of the leaves of *Tetragonia cornuta* which eats as well as spinage'.

Cook took seeds of *Tetragonia* back to England where there are accounts of it being grown in nineteenth century kitchen gardens.

In Asia, Chinese spinach is yet another genus – *Amaranthus dubius* – and Ceylon spinach – Basella – is now cultivated in Africa and tropical America. *Atriplex hortensis* is the orache or spinach of Central Asia.

Obviously the sun-king knew a good thing when he tasted it and in choosing a vegetable with world-wide local appeal Popeye showed a remarkable sense of marketing.

Previously unpublished.

Quandongs

Bush Tucker Man is focussing our attention on the new taste sensations offered by our native flora and there is some commercial evidence of this increasing interest.

It is fascinating to dig deep among the packets of a well-known brand of Australian jelly in the supermarkets to find flavours like Lilli-pilli, Minjinberry and Quandong. There is no doubting this quandong is *Eleocarpus grandis*. The resulting jelly is so blue it would camouflage a host of smurfees!

There are two quandongs native to Australia. *Eleocarpus grandis* – the blue quandong of the coastal rainforests of Queensland and northern New South Wales – and *Santalum acuminatum* – the quandong, or native peach, of warm temperate areas.

The fruit of *Santalum acuminatum* was familiar to early settlers in the southern parts of Australia. They used it for jams, relishes and pie fillings. J. H. Maiden, director of the Sydney Botanic Gardens, in 1889 likened its flavour to that of the Black Guava.

Aborigines enjoyed the kernels of the quandong which are singularly rich in oil and some enthusiasts consider them a prospective alternative to the macadamia.

For the past twelve years CSIRO has been monitoring selected seedlings of *Santalum acuminatum* on a property near Quorn in South Australia. The horticultural importance of these trees has led the South Australian branch of the National Trust to list the Quorn Quandongs in that state's register of significant trees.

Previously unpublished.

The iris

One of the oldest cultivated plants in history, the iris is depicted on the walls of the temple at Karnak and in a fresco at the Palace of Minos at Knossos. It often decorated the brow of the Sphinx as its three petals were said to signify faith, wisdom and valour.

The plant takes its name from the Greek goddess, Iris, who used the rainbow as a pathway to earth where the flowers that bear her name were believed to grow from her footprints.

Renaissance painters associated the iris with the birth of Christ. Look carefully at Leonardo da Vinci's *Madonna of the Rocks*, and Durer's *Virgin and Child*. In Hugo van der Goes' *Adorazione* you can identify the species *Iris florentina* and *I. pallida*.

The sixteenth century Flemish triptych in the Melbourne Arts Centre has a superbly painted example of *I. trojana*. Ladies in China and Japan used the powdered roots of *I. tectorum* for whitening their skin. The flower was grown on the thatched roofs of Japanese houses to avoid wasting land needed for crops. In China and Japan, stylised forms of *I. ensata* and *I. laevigata* can be seen in embroidery and lacquer work designs.

In Japan's samurai past, *I. japonica* was planted on the steep slopes leading to feudal

castles. The slippery foliage had any advancing army skidding in reverse and subject to easy repulse from the parapets.

French armies fleeing before the invading Goths had reason to thank the clumps of yellow flags, *Iris pseudacorus*, that indicated shallow water and safe passage across the River Lys.

Thereafter, King Clovis chose the water iris as his badge – his 'fleur de lys' – and Louis VII adopted the same emblem but he referred to it as the 'fleur de Louis'.

The English botanist, William Turner, wrote of the 'fleur delice' in his *New Herball* of 1551, while John Parkinson speaks of *I. variegata* as 'the yellow variable flower de luce' – the flower of light – in his *Paradisus* of 1629.

Medieval monks recognised the medicinal properties of the iris plant prescribing it for ulcers and to induce sleep. Over the centuries orris powder, pounded from the dried rhizomes of *I. florentina, I. pallida* and *I. germanica*, has been a perfume for linen, a sweetener for rinses, a scent for soap, toothpaste and shampoo. To-day, many know it as a fixative in pot-pourri.

The name Dykes is synonymous with iris. W. R. Dykes, a master at Charterhouse School in England, became an expert on the genus both in a practical and a botanic sense. He grew every variety of iris he could obtain and in 1913 published a monumental work *The Genus Iris* illustrated by F. H. Round.

An Australian artist-cum-educationist, Winifred West, was also inspired by the iris. To her it exemplified the beauty she wished to create at Frensham, the school she established at Mittagong. Frensham has the iris as its badge and the iris colours – mauve, green, brown and gold – as school colours.

Through the work of hybridisers like Barry Blythe of Tempo Two, Australia is establishing a reputation overseas for producing reliable cultivars. Success in the Italian Primo Firenze competition has further enhanced Australia's horticultural achievement.

Respect for the subtle beauty of the iris promises to stretch as far into the future as it has already done in the past.

Previously unpublished.

Geraniums and pelargoniums

Flowers are often so much part of our habitual landscape that we do not notice them until they are not there. Yet when you unexpectedly come upon some flower in a foreign place, *mal de pays* strikes swiftly and surely.

In the provincial French town of Pau, I discovered that geraniums were rooted in the landscape of my Australian childhood. Not geraniums carefully cultivated in pots of greenhouses, but straggly, dusty geraniums under a bleached summer sky.

Australians should acknowledge the geranium in the Bicentennial celebration. Among the cultivated exotics it reigned supreme in what passed for the gardens of colonial New South Wales.

In autumn 1770, Joseph Banks and Dr Daniel Solander found geraniums in the area of Botany Bay. They recorded their finds as *Geranium pilosum* (later known as *G. solanderi*) and *G. australe* (later *Pelargonium australe*).

One of the first South African botanic discoveries to reach England and flower there (in John Tradescant's garden) was recorded in the 1633 edition of Gerard's *Herball* as *Geranium indicum odoratum, flore maculo*, a name which suggested that it came from India or the Indies. In

reality it was the humble, sand-loving *Pelargonium triste*, native to the Cape of Good Hope.

It was not until 1789 that a botanist, Charles l'Heretier, designated the genus *Pelargonium* as distinct from the genus *Geranium*.

Pelargonium capitatum, indigenous to South Africa, naturalised and spread in the Australian colonies. One view is that its seeds arrived in Australia on the coats of stock which were off-loaded at Capetown for a period of agistment before their long voyage across the Indian Ocean.

Others suggest that the seeds may have been transported in the Cape sand that was taken aboard as ballast for the passage through the roaring forties. Sand from wrecked ships was washed ashore bearing the pelargonium seed to germinate when it reached dry land.

Either way, *P. capitatum* established itself and thrived on the shores of Botany Bay and is still seen on the Kurnell peninsula.

The fine distinction between geraniums and pelargoniums was lost on the early settlers of New South Wales. The captain of a ship visiting Sydney Town wrote:

> *Geraniums flourish in such abundance that ... they are made into hedges ... they are always in leaf and flower and emit an odour of the most fragrant nature.*

What were described as geraniums might well have been pelargoniums as the Darling Nursery, established in 1826 by Thomas Shepherd at the behest of Governor Darling, included pelargoniums in its catalogue.

Mrs Charles Meredith noted in the 1840s that 'Geraniums thrive and grow rapidly but I do not see any good ones; none that I would have thought worth cultivating in England'.

There was a prospect of better things to come. She continued 'A Horticultural Society has now been established some years and will doubtless be the means of much improvement.'

When the *Horticultural Society Magazine* of the 1860s

described a visit to Mr Robert Henderson's Camellia Grove Nursery at Newtown, the praise was rather faint – 'Of course we do not wish it to be thought that our Mr Henderson at present is anything near equal to home [meaning English] growers, but he is gradually improving our stock of that estimable plant, the pelargonium.'

In fact, however, the named cultivars at the nursery – 'Hobart Town', 'Maid of Tasmania', 'Mayor of Melbourne' and 'Pride of St Kilda' – suggested that local hybridisation was occurring.

By the end of the century, inland from Gulgong, Henry Lawson had Joe Wilson observe

> *Geraniums were the only flowers I saw grow in the drought out there. I remembered this woman had a few dirty grey-green leaves behind some sticks against the bark wall near the door ...*

and the classic short-story 'Water Them Geraniums' became part of Australian literature.

To be precise, we should recognise geraniums and pelargoniums as the mainstay of our early garden heritage.

Previously unpublished.

The Douglas Fir

The Douglas Fir (*Pseudotsuga taxifolia*) is an impressive conifer of the mountain areas of Washington, Oregon, California and Arizona. Fully grown it can tower three hundred feet and measure forty feet in circumference. Masses of soft, dark, aromatic needles cover the branches which bear the egg-shaped cones. The bark is thick, corky and deeply grooved. Growth is relatively fast – one hundred feet in less than thirty years – and the resulting wood is strong, durable and straight-grained. In a developing country like nineteenth century America timber from the Douglas Fir was used for bridges, railroad sleepers and wagons, telegraph poles, house-building, boardwalks and ships. Originally discovered by Archibald Menzies, a naval surgeon and amateur botanist, the tree was popularly named in recognition of David Douglas who really introduced the tree to the world in 1827.

When Americans of the 1820s were on the threshold of their great westward thrust, a remarkable young Scot, David Douglas, joined those trekking towards a 'manifest destiny'. Douglas was searching for new plants rather than cheap land but he, too, was caught up in the optimism of frontier exploration.

In 1823 the Horticultural Society of London had appointed the twenty-four-year-old Douglas a plant collector in the eastern United States. On his first American visit he attended the gala opening of the Erie Canal at Albany, New York, visited Joseph Bonaparte's house in Louisiana and saw the Niagara Falls. Douglas travelled by stage coach, horse-drawn canal barge and paddle steamer. Compared with his later modes of transport, his introductory expeditions were civilised indeed.

Whenever and however he travelled, David Douglas cared

only for his plant collections. His baggage included seeds, dried specimens, living plants and, most importantly, meticulous records of plant distributions and habitats. The West lured Douglas time after time. Successive trips saw him pushing further towards the unexplored areas of the Columbia River, California, Canada and Alaska.

Obsessed with botanical research, Douglas preferred thirty quires of paper (for drying and packing his specimens) to extra clothing when preparing to go into the Rocky Mountain area where he would face the challenge of rushing streams and deep snowdrifts. Although the Chinook Indians befriended him, calling him 'the Grass Man', Douglas met other Indians who were decidedly unfriendly.

Privation became commonplace and near starvation once drove Douglas to eat the berries and seeds he had so painfully collected. He also recounted how he was twice obliged to eat his horse. Like the American waggoners, he not only faced natural dangers but he suffered fevers, eye trouble, plagues of fleas and attacks by ants. With characteristic stoicism he wrote in his diary:

> ... travelled thirty three miles, drenched and bleached with rain and sleet, chilled with a piercing north wind, and to finish the day experienced the cooling, comfortless consolation of lying down wet without fire or supper. On such occasions I am very liable to become fretful.

The period in the Oregon Territory produced the conifer collections for which Douglas is best known: notably *Pseudotsuga taxifolia*, the tree popularly known as the Douglas Fir, and the Sugar Pine, the search for which nearly cost him his life several times over in the face of Indians, storms, hunger and grizzly bears. Undaunted, Douglas set out for Hudson Bay, a journey of 10,000 miles which took more than two years on foot with pack-horse.

On his return to London in 1827, Douglas was elected a Fellow of the Linnaean Society, the Zoological Society and the Geological Society but these tokens of esteem were not matched in any material way. He grew increasingly disgruntled with London and he sailed for California in 1829. This time Douglas had impressive patrons. The British Colonial Office, the Royal Navy, the Hudson Bay Company, the Horticultural Society and the Zoological Society all supported him.

Initially he headed for the less rugged sections of the Pacific coast. The Mexican-controlled area with its Spanish cultural influence delighted the botanist. He became 'Don David', the respected acquaintance of many Franciscan missionaries who sympathised with his scientific work. In California, he found the Garrya and he sent specimens of the Monterey Pine and annuals such as Wild Heliotrope, Blazing Star and the Californian Bluebell back to England. Douglas also sent plants to the Botanic Gardens in St Petersburg where it is alleged specks of gold were seen in the accompanying soil. Russia supported Douglas when financial vicissitudes beset the Horticultural Society. Russian interest led him to attempt field work in Alaska but ill-fortune dogged the expedition. His canoe capsized in the rapids at Fort George Canyon and Douglas lost four hundred specimens as well as all notes on the Californian botanic work.

Depressed, Douglas determined to return to London via the Hawaiian Islands. Botanising in these Pacific islands cheered him but in 1834 when he was planning his journey back home he was gored to death by a wild bull following a fall into a pit-trap near Hilo.

The Douglas Fir is a lasting memorial for the solitary, rugged Scot whose indomitable will challenged the hazards of frontier life and extended botanic knowledge.

Previously unpublished.

Trees for the swagman and the smith

Poetry has positioned many a folk hero under a shady tree. In America, New England to be precise, Longfellow's blacksmith enjoyed the protection of the spreading chestnut tree, while in Australia, Paterson's jolly swagman relished the shade of the coolibah tree.

Strangely each of these trees has been imported to the other country. The coolibah (*Eucalyptus microtheca*), a hardy species which stoically copes with drought, frost and flood, has been planted quite widely in Arizona where its shade is appreciated in summer.

Early settlers in Australia realised that the coolibah, with a luxuriant crown of foliage, was a sign of water. In some parts of the country *E. microtheca* is known as the Flooded Box, although the species name refers to the unusually small gumnut it produces.

Item No. 194 in the South Australian National Trust's register of significant trees is the Coolibah Tree of Innamincka. Growing on the bank of Cooper Creek, this coolibah became the cenotaph for Robert O'Hara Burke. His bones were found in its shade by search party leader A. W. Howitt. On the trunk of the tree Howitt inscribed:

R.O.H.B.
21.9.61 [1861]

The drifting sand of the desert has kept the epitaph intact for more than a century.

The precise species of Longfellow's chestnut is open to speculation. English and European readers assume it to be *Castanea sativa* (the European or Spanish chestnut), whereas some botanical purists might claim it to be *C. dentata* (the American chestnut).

Ironically, the disease Endothia parasitica gained a footing in 1904 and within forty years killed the American chestnuts of Eastern America.

Those who show today's tourists the site of Longfellow's smithy point to a fine *C. sativa* and indeed it is possible that one of the early settlers in New England planted the exotic species which would have had ample time to reach maturity before Longfellow penned his verses.

The edible seed of *C. dentata* has given it a richer history than that of *E. microtheca*. Legend claims that the European chestnut (*C. sativa*) reached western Europe from the Middle East through Castan, a town in eastern Thessaly which is commemorated in the generic name.

Ancient Romans were partial to chestnuts and Caesar's legions undoubtedly spread them throughout Europe. The longevity of the chestnut tree is exemplified by the story of the famous tree on Mount Etna which was said to have been planted by Romans in the second century BC. It attained a girth of 204 feet before its destruction by volcanic eruption in 1850.

In the long run the coolibah may prove more resistant to natural disaster and disease than the mighty chestnut and so build up its place in Australian folk and plant lore.

Previously unpublished.

Gardens

Gardens: introduction

Nina Crone was an indefatigable traveller. Perhaps this was destined, as her father had been a professional sea captain. Her first major journey was undertaken at the age of four, when the family travelled from England to settle in Australia.

On completion of her undergraduate studies at the University of Melbourne, Nina travelled to Europe where she gained an appreciation for garden styles and vistas. As her professional life became increasingly busy, travel, her interest in gardens and writing about them were her form of relaxation.

Every opportunity to combine her professional and extra-curricular interests was grasped. During holiday periods, foreign study tours with other school principals, or international tours with her students, she took advantage of spare moments to visit parks and gardens. Before departure, she carefully researched the places she was to visit. Wherever she went, she collected postcards and brochures, took many photographs or slides, and wrote copious diary entries, detailing the places she visited and her impressions.

Nina used her written notes, and the guide books and postcards she collected, to write the articles for *The Age* that are featured in this section. Her reassuring style, based on sound knowledge and understanding, inspired faith in her readers, allowing them to share her interest and pleasure. The fascinating history of the development of the gardens she wrote about, the snapshots of pleasant corners in which to spend time, and her depictions of splendid walks and vistas were all written to entice the people of Melbourne to seek out gardens in far corners of the world or interstate. For those who had no hope of making such journeys, simply reading Nina's delightful descriptions of gardens in Britain, Europe, Asia, the United States, and Australia could transport them there from their breakfast tables, enabling them to share in the unfailing joy Nina derived from her botanical journeyings.

Helen Botham

A world of contrasts waits in the Big Apple

This is the first of an occasional series by ALISON DALRYMPLE on interstate and overseas gardens, particularly public gardens. The series will advise travellers what to look for; and stimulate ideas about what can be done in Melbourne. The first is about a garden in New York; the next will be about one in China.

BROOKLYN BOTANIC GARDENS, NEW YORK. Established: 1910; Area: 50 acres; Highlights: variety of mini-gardens, Children's Garden, Japanese Gardens, reference library for gardeners. Satellite Gardens: Teatown and Kitchawan.

O f the many areas in the Brooklyn Botanic Gardens none contrasts more than the Children's Garden and the Japanese Gardens. Meandering pumpkin vines, rows of maize, showy sunflowers, full-blown roses and cheerful noise characterise the Children's Garden. Tranquillity mirroring nature is the essence of the Japanese Landscape Garden.

Entering the gardens by the Flatbush Avenue gate the visitor comes to the section of the Children's Garden where plants mentioned in Shakespeare's writings spill in profusion over flagged paths. There is a generous carelessness reminiscent of the English cottage garden: lady smocks (*Cardomine pratensis*), cuckoo buds (*Ranunculus acris*), crown imperials (*Fritillaria imperialis*), honey stalks (*Trifolium pratense* or *Trifolium repens*), love-in-

Shakespeare Garden, part of the Brooklyn Botanic Garden, New York. Photographer: Nina Crone.

idleness (*Viola tricolor*), marybuds (*Calendula officinalis*), rosemary (*Rosmarinus officinalis*), rue (*Ruta graveolens*) and sweet eglantine (*Rose eglanteria*). It is a garden sensitive to history, literature and botany: a romantic corner for dreaming in the summer sunshine.

> *I know a bank where the wild thyme blows,*
> *Where oxlips and the nodding violet grows*
> *Quite over-canopied with luscious woodbine,*
> *With sweet musk roses and with eglantine.*

Next door there is action. Nine-year-olds are tending cabbages or chasing butterflies. They have worked through the season following a predetermined planting plan. The 14-year-olds have developed their own plot, selecting vegetables from a list – cucumbers, beans, tomatoes and turnips. Initially at least no one worries about Latin names.

About 300 children participate in a program which begins with theoretical explanations and indoor demonstrations during late winter. Teachers from the Brooklyn Gardens staff work with the children planning and preparing for April planting. Friends share an allotment and are jointly responsible for maintaining it. By autumn the children are weighing and photographing their produce. The sense of achievement and spirit of co-operation confirm the value of the Children's Garden in an urban community.

Children's Garden (from Nina's booklet, *Brooklyn Botanic Garden –* undated). Courtesy of Brooklyn Botanic Garden, bbg.org

Japanese garden forms are well represented in Brooklyn Botanic. There is a *hojo* or flat garden, a *roji* or dewy path garden, a dwarf plant garden, a bonsai collection and a hill-and-pond or landscape garden.

Dewy path gardens evolved in the Middle Ages. They represent the most refined and condensed form of Japanese garden, aiming to create the feeling of a remote mountain wilderness by making a narrow border from stones and selected plants which thrive under

moist or dewy conditions – lichens, mosses and ferns.
Accustomed to boundless acres and distant horizons, Australians often miss the miniaturised scale of the *roji* garden in Brooklyn. It leads to and from the replica of the Roanji Temple stone garden.

Established in 1914–15, the Hill-and-Pond Garden is one of the world's most beautiful strolling gardens. The scale of the garden, the symbolic significance of its elements, the tranquillity of its vistas, whatever the season, all encourage relaxation and meditation. The feeling of an entire landscape almost within one's reach is achieved by artful pruning. Shrubs are sheared into rounded shapes to suggest hills and some are pruned so that their foliage masses suggest clouds. Pines are trained to look small, old and windswept.

The flowing shape of the lake is taken from the Chinese character for heart or mind; the rocks symbolise quietness, timelessness and stability. Pines are the predominant trees symbolising longevity. A *torii* leading to a shrine, a drum bridge, stone lanterns, willows and stepping stones enhance the water views. Flowers are used with restraint – apricot and cherry blooms, a few azaleas, wistaria by the cascades and iris by the lake.

There are many more specialist gardens in the Brooklyn Botanic – herb, rose, iris, cherry, magnolia, water-lily, rhododendron, fragrance and local flora. All justify Brooklyn's fame as 'many gardens within a garden'.

The Age, Friday 24 August 1984, Weekender, p. 7.

Extract from Nina's travel diary

16 August 1980

Got off at busy corner of Ocean Drive and Flatbush Avenue to visit Brooklyn Botanic Gardens – well worth it. Small but carefully planned. The first impression was through the Children's Garden, an interesting scheme of organised and supervised allotments meshed into a study program on several levels with a special house as a Centre.

The occasional man
fancies himself in paradise

HANGZHOU BOTANIC GARDENS. Established 1956; Area: 252 hectares; Highlights: medicinal herb garden, bamboo garden, garden of ornamental plants, plant classification centre, garden of endangered species.

So many pleasures are to be found here, wrote Marco Polo of Hangzhou[1] in the late 13th century, 'that man fancies himself to be in paradise'. Some of the gardens he saw in the region of Xihu (West Lake) remain a pleasure for today's visitors to China.

Ancient Chinese gardens were the work of poets, scholars and monks who contemplated the landscape and then created a garden as they would a painting with the elements of rock, water and plant. Compared with the great European and English gardens, classical Chinese gardens are small and superbly proportioned. Against this tradition, the idea of comprehensive botanic gardens seems discordant.

To visit Wuxi and not see the Li Garden with its grotesque rockeries, bow bridges, covered promenade and 89 differently designed windows is to miss the legend of a local king who planned the garden to court a princess. To visit Suzhou and not see Cang Lan Ting (the Surging Wave Pavilion), Liu Yuan (the Tarrying Garden) or Zhuozheng Yuan (the Humble Administrator's Garden) is to miss the epitome of Chinese garden design; and to visit Hangzhou and not see the Botanic Gardens is to miss something of the contemporary People's Republic of China.

---

1 Hangzhou was misspelt as 'Hangchou' in the original article in *The Age* and has been corrected here.

Within a year of the 1949 Revolution Zhejiang province was planning botanic gardens at Hangzhou in recognition of the educational, research and conservation needs of the country. A site at Taoyuanling close to the West Lake offered suitable topography, good water supply and adequate communication links with the city.

A special nursery began the collection of seeds while experts from Beijing, Nanjing and Shanghai worked with provincial botanists to develop the general plan of the gardens. In 1956 construction started. Nine years later, growth was well established and the gardens were opened to the public.

Covering 250 hectares, the gardens have two greenhouses and nearly 3500 taxa. Special collections include *Acer, Camellia, Carpinus, Cinnamon, Dioscorea, Magnolia, Osmanthus, Phyllostachys, Rhododendron* and *Rosa*.

In making botanic gardens there is the temptation to include as much as is physically possible and 20 years is hardly time for the essence of a garden to emerge. It is the enormous variety and range of specimens which give the Hangzhou Botanic Gardens their appeal.

Confronted with an embarrassment of riches the visitor must select preferred areas of interest. The time of year will influence choice, of course, but whatever the season garden-lovers should

Melbourne Church of England Girls Grammar School China tour group and guides at Hangzhou Gardens in 1984. Photographer: Helen Forgasz.

seek out the garden of landscape, the bamboo garden and the garden of sweet osmanthus and crepe myrtle.

Botanists will relish the collection of rare and endangered species from Zhoushan Island and from Zhejiang – *Carpinus putoensis, Neolitsia sericea, Calycanthus chinensis, Pseudotaxus chienii* and *Heptocodium jasminoides*. Those interested in herbal medicines will enjoy the specimens displayed in a corridor commemorating Li Shizhen, a physician of the Ming dynasty.

These gardens offer escape from the throngs of people always found trekking an appreciative course through the classical gardens of China. Understandably, Chinese young people like the rhododendron groves which afford space for quiet courtship. The Hangzhou Botanic Gardens provide a delightful foil to the classic landscape gardens of Suzhou and Wuxi as well as representing the horticultural face of post-revolutionary China.

NOTE: Madame Gu Xiuliang, governor of Jiangsu province, which is the 'sister state' to Victoria, visited Melbourne this year [1984]. She believes the establishment of a Chinese garden here will further friendship and cultural understanding between Australia and China.

The Age, 5 October 1984, Weekender, p. 7.

Italians savor a Scotsman's legacy

VILLA TARANTO BOTANICAL GARDENS, PALLANZA, ITALY. Established: 1931; Area: 20 hectares; Highlights: terrace gardens, valletta, tree fern glade, antiquities, fountains and pools.

A rrival by water enhances a visit to any garden, so it is little wonder that the Italian lakes are rimmed with remarkable gardens like those of Isola Bella or Villa Taranto on Lake Maggiore.

In 1931 a Scotsman, Captain Neil McEachern, bought a property on the Castagnolan promontory near Pallanza. His ambition was to create one of the best botanical gardens in the world. He began landscape works by excavating a spectacular 'valletta' and constructing an irrigation system which feeds waterfalls, fills lily and lotus pools and supplies ornamental fountains and watersprays.

McEachern amassed more than 20,000 species from all over the world, first acclimatising them and then planting them artfully to enhance his vistas. He established his own laboratory to assist his seed collecting and propagation.

By making a garden in Europe, McEachern was emulating Englishmen like the Marquis of Hertford who, in 1835, bought Bagatelle in Paris and whose son, Sir Richard Wallace, built and maintained a spectacular garden there.

Private botanical gardens have particular qualities. Often there is a feeling of over-indulgence, a surfeit of care, a degree of theatricality about them. Certainly there is a dramatic beauty in Villa Taranto's setting: the backdrop of mountains and the foreground of shining water.

The entrance drive edged by lawn and pines is memorable. It leads up a hill giving glimpses of the tree-fern glade, the

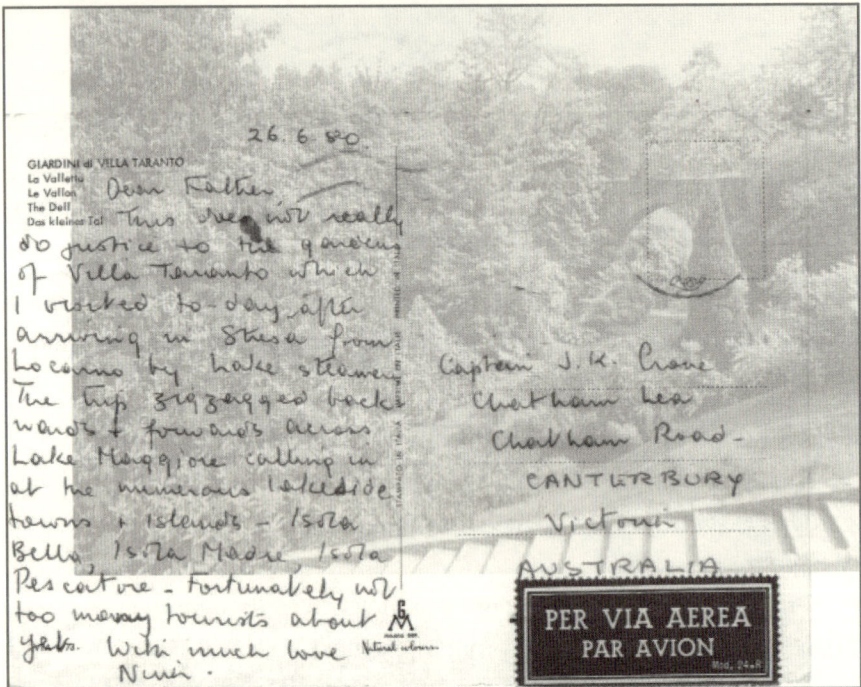

GIARDINI di VILLA TARANTO
La Valletta
Le Vallon
The Dell
Das kleines Tal

26.6.80

Dear Kathie,
This does not really
do justice to the gardens
of Villa Taranto which
I visited to-day after
arriving in Stresa from
Locarno by lake steamer.
The trip zig zagged back-
wards + forwards across
Lake Maggiore calling in
at the numerous lakeside
towns + islands — Isola
Bella, Isola Madre, Isola
Pescatore. Fortunately not
too many tourists about
yet. With much love
Nina.

Captain J. K. Crone
Chatham Lea
Chatham Road,
CANTERBURY
Victoria
AUSTRALIA

PER VIA AEREA
PAR AVION
Mod. 24.8

Nina's postcard to her father (26 June 1980). Courtesy Administration of the Botanical Gardens of Villa Taranto (for image reproduction).

cherub fountain, the Italian garden and a magnificent princess tree (*Paulownia tomentosa*). A detour leads to the glasshouse where the gigantic lily-pads of *Victoria amazonica* attract a constant stream of visitors.

On high ground, overlooking the man-made valley, the rhododendron wood provides a glowing display in April and May, while on the opposite side of the path magnolias and later paeonies, pick up the pink and white theme. From the steps, which lead up to the villa itself, there is a view into the valletta where the April-flowering handkerchief tree (*Davidia involucrata*) creates a focus of interest.

Northwest of the main lawn is the oldest part of the gardens. Here, two splendid beech trees (*Fagus sylvatica* 'asplenifolia' and *F. sylvatica* 'ëpendula') are dominant. Nearby, banks of azaleas face a grove of cedars and the area is also interesting for a thriving example of *Camellia sinensis* (the tea plant).

A graceful viaduct bridges the valletta, bringing visitors to the pergola. In June this is rich with the slightly fragrant, white *Rosa soulieana*. The elegant terrace gardens with their symmetry, colorful display beds, clipped lawn and serene pools epitomise McEachern's planning. A charming bronze, 'Il Pescatore' patiently waits to catch a fish in full view of the villa itself.

Among the trees bordering the Terrace Garden are some attractive specimens: *Trachycarpus fortunei*, *Fagus sylvatica* '*Purpurea*', *Cornus florida* '*Rubra*' and *Quercus coccinea*. Further up the hill above the Terrace Garden visitors with specialist interests will find the bog garden, the erica garden, the lily ponds, the maple grove, the cotoneaster collection and the conifers planted by famous people.

Discreetly sited amidst the trees on the hillside are many antiquities. There is a staircase of Etruscan amphorae, an excavated statue of 'Pan and Ninfa', and an archaeological road in the process of development. That these in no way intrude on the cultivated beauty of the hillside once again evidences McEachern's supreme sense of balance and harmony.

It is just over 20 years since Captain McEachern died, leaving his property to the Italian State as a school of gardening. The task of maintaining and preserving this one-man botanical garden has been faithfully honored.

More than 175,000 people enjoy the incomparable beauty of the gardens between April and October each year – a telling compliment to the man who created the Giardini di Villa Taranto.

The Age, 26 October 1984, Weekender, p. 7.

America's most civilised acres

DUMBARTON OAKS, GEORGETOWN, WASHINGTON, DC. Established: 1800 (house), 1920s (gardens); Area: 16 acres; Highlights: terrace gardens, herbaceous borders, vista and prospect, orangery, maple and box walks, historic gardens, library, music, art and conference centre.

What's in a name? In the case of Dumbarton Oaks, many things. As a child in wartime I first heard of it as the venue for discussion of the establishment of the United Nations Organisation.

Stravinsky's 'Dumbarton Oaks' concerto reminded me it was a centre for music. Its collection of Byzantine art led me to expect a fine museum. But the garden was an unanticipated joy, discovered on a late summer visit to Washington, DC.

There is year-round interest in the garden. Evergreens, coniferous and broad-leafed predominate, although deciduous trees and shrubs form a frame for the flowers. These subtly emphasise the monochromatic effect. The overwhelming impression is verdure and serenity.

Behind the green creepers, beneath the ivy ground cover, is the solidity of stone and brick. Inscribed in much of the stone is the wisdom of the ages written in Latin or Chaucerian English. Man's intellect and nature's bounty have made Dumbarton Oaks what it is today – a centre for symposia and study.

The purchase of the property by career diplomat Robert Woods Bliss in 1920 arose from his wish for 'a country house in the city'.

The distinguished landscape gardener, Beatrix Jones Farrand, worked on the formal design of the garden. Her task was challenging as the Blisses were overseas for the first 10 years of ownership. Her achievement was masterly.

The north court, enclosed by the wings of the drawing room and the music room, faces the north vista, where three rectangular lawns on different levels descend to a 'prospect' above a steep drop. From here, only sky and the trees of the hillside on the other side of the valley are visible.

From the terrace of the 'green garden' steps pass a baroque fountain and lead on to the swimming pool terrace with its wistaria-covered loggia. At the western end, a wall fountain shaded by weeping cherries is backed by a superb cedar. The swimming pool itself reflects the green foliage of willows.

At the eastern end of the green garden there is a series of formal terraces. The beech terrace surrounds a silver-stemmed beech beneath which a pink marble table and benches provide a delightful conversation area.

The urn terrace has attractive beds of dwarf shamrock-leafed ivy, surrounding pebble areas in which the central urn is set. Beds of paeonies, columbines and irises partially screen the

The Fountain Terrace, Dumbarton Oaks. Courtesy of Dumbarton Oaks Research Library.

open-work brick balustrade along which wistaria and winter jasmine are growing.

The rose terrace, with specimen box hedges and rose beds, leads to the fountain terrace by double staircase. To the north is the original herb garden, now converted into a pot garden with a wistaria-covered arbor.

Below the terraces, paths wind down the hillside in various directions to points of interest – herbaceous borders framed by yew trees, the cutting and kitchen gardens and, about 18 metres below the beech terrace, a natural glade with a pool. Beyond this is a walk where a double line of silver maples forms an arcade leading to a meadow. In spring this is a riot of cherry blossom, bulbs and forsythia.

In 1940 Robert and Mildred Bliss willed Dumbarton Oaks to Harvard University and the lower wilderness slopes of the property were set aside as a public area, Dumbarton Oaks Park.

Later, Mrs Bliss devoted her collecting interests to the

Extract from a letter

To Tommy Garnett, Editor of the Gardening section of *The Age*, 6 November 1984:

Here is another trio of offerings, including the Dumbarton Oaks article.

Thank you for your suggestion that you lend me a book to refresh my memory. I relied on notes from my travel diary but as you can see, on the occasion of my visit, I was more interested in the history of the property than in the botanical specimens in the gardens. Consequently, I feel the piece is very light on information and individual plants. What really impressed me was the culture and intellect behind the planning of the garden. In the Terrace Gardens everything was so rational, so civilised. Such a contrast with the romantic elements of the 'wild' garden in the valley (now the public park). Should your book have more specific detail of the plantings, and should you prefer the article to have more horticultural emphasis, I will be happy to re-work the piece with the assistance of your book.

---

enlargement and improvement of the garden library, which contains early botanical works and treatises – *Hortus sanitatis* of 1492, the *Materia Medica* of Dioscorides, dated 1499, and the first edition of *Gerard's Herball* of 1597.

Seminars and symposia on garden history and botanical subjects are held in this unique setting and the papers are published under the Dumbarton Oaks label and distributed throughout the world. Subject matter has included Persian gardens, Roman gardens and the English 'landscape' gardens.

Dumbarton Oaks with its music room, its libraries, its Byzantine and pre-Columbian art, and its gardens and parks has been called 'America's most civilised square mile'. Garden enthusiasts the world over, whatever their specialty, are exceptionally well served by this remarkable centre.

The Age, 30 November 1984, Weekender, p. 7.

Bagatelle it may be, but it is no mere rose garden

The French, as much as the English, love roses. The names Bourbon, Redouté, Malmaison and Meilland prove it. Each summer Parisians flock to Bagatelle to see the roses, but few foreign visitors know these delightful gardens.

Modern Bagatelle dates from 1777 when the Comte d'Artois wagered that he could speedily rebuild a lodge he owned in the Bois de Boulogne. He won his bet when the building was completed in 64 days. Nine hundred workmen had toiled night and day while Swiss Guards hijacked cartloads of the necessary building materials.

The Comte adopted the fashionable English landscape style for his property, employing Thomas Blaikie, a Scot, as gardener. Blaikie kept a detailed diary which makes interesting reading:

Wednesday, 30 December 1778: Began the gardens of Bagatelle by dividing the wood in front of the pavilion to open up a lawn with the help of M. Brias, Inspector of Buildings, but he was surprised to see me draw up this garden without cord or dividers. He did not come back.

Thursday, 31 December 1778: It is strange to state that people here have no taste for perspective. They think that the house and garden are two distinct elements without any relationship to each other.

Thomas Blaikie achieved a great deal at Bagatelle. He improved the soil by bringing alluvial soil from the nearby banks of the Seine and he set up a reservoir for the property.

After the French Revolution and the First Empire, the Marquis of Hertford bought Bagatelle and his natural son, Sir Richard Wallace, inherited the estate in 1870.

The Marquis of Hertford's French gardener, Vare, created a great expanse of lawn surrounded by winding paths and enhanced by a lake with grottoes and waterfalls. The orangery and some rustic chalets near the orchard and kitchen garden were built by Sir Richard Wallace, who maintained the elegant grounds with the assistance of 20 gardeners.

After Wallace's death there was talk of sub-division. Happily, the City of Paris purchased the property and incorporated it into the Bois de Boulogne. Bagatelle was preserved as a souvenir of the 18th century and as an example of the evolution of a garden.

The Rose Garden, established in 1903 on a field where once the Marquis of Hertford arranged daily riding practice for the son of Napoleon III, is a symmetrical garden screened by ancient oaks. It contains a comprehensive collection of roses all carefully documented with name, origin and date of planting. There are 7000 roses and 684 different varieties – 178 polyanthas and floribundas, 378 Hybrid Teas, 92 weeping varieties, 14 shrub varieties and 200 new varieties.

The Concours International of new roses was the idea of Jules Gravereaux, who had created the rose garden at *l'Hay les Roses*, and of J. C. N. Forestier, the Keeper of Paris Parks and Gardens in the early years of this century.

In spring 1907, new varieties of roses collected from French and overseas rosarians were planted at Bagatelle. The Paris Municipal Council decided to create an international competition among the new roses and donated a gold medal. The Concours captured the imagination of growers and public alike. Today, there is not only a gold medal, but two silver medals, two certificates and a cup for scented roses.

The rose bushes from French and foreign growers are planted in a special section of the Rose Garden reserved for the competition. The soil is replenished only after exhaustive scientific analysis to ensure that all competitors have an equal chance. Bush roses are cultivated for two years, climbing roses for three.

The gardener responsible for the Rose Garden notes, on individual labels, the number of flowers produced by each variety during each season. A commission examines the plants for vigor, resistance to disease, perfume and the aggregate of flowers.

The jury examines the new varieties and its judgment is added to that of the commission. The rules of the competition are rigorous and the anonymity of the roses and their breeders is maintained until the announcement of results, when a sealed envelope, submitted with the original rose for planting and given a number, is matched with the number of the rose judged best. The envelope is opened and the name of the prize-winning rose and its creator become public.

The Concours provides new stock for Bagatelle's Rose Garden and a focus for visitors who return again and again. A June afternoon spent viewing the roses, drinking coffee on the outdoor terrace and watching Parisians admire their gardens is an unforgettable experience.

The Age, Friday 28 December 1984, Weekender, p. 5.

Rose Garden, Bagatelle, Paris. Photographer: Nina Crone.

The Desert Garden, Huntington, 'the best I have seen anywhere' (Nina's travel diary, 16 September 1980). Photographer: James Hitchmough.

The Heather Garden, Royal Botanical Garden, Edinburgh. Photographer: Nina Crone.

The marble-lined pool of the Patio de la Acequia – the Courtyard of the Long Pool, Generalife, Granada. Photographer: Nina Crone.

Kitchen garden at Mount Vernon. Courtesy of the Mount Vernon Ladies' Association.

Cooks' Cottage vegetable garden, Fitzroy Gardens, Melbourne, in 2008. Photographer: Helen Botham.

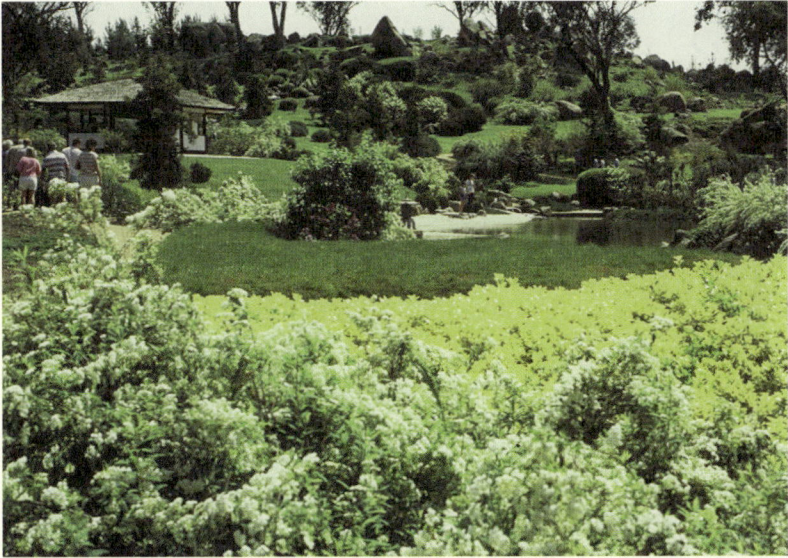

Lake, teahouse and stone lantern, Cowra Japanese Garden, New South Wales. Photographer: Nina Crone.

Chinese Garden of Friendship, Darling Harbour, Sydney, in 2008. Photographer: Brenda Joyce.

Railroaders' riches spawned a marvel of botany

There are moments when trends sweep nations. Like the time in the early 1900s when the United States, led by that rumbustious President Teddy Roosevelt, discovered conservation and natural resources. The frontier had well and truly closed as railroads criss-crossed the continent making millionaires of their owners.

The conjunction of a railroad, fortune and a philanthropic endeavor, directed towards botanic knowledge, left the world a remarkable heritage – the Huntington[1] Botanic Gardens.

Like much else in Los Angeles, Huntington is large-scale. Landscaped gardens now cover 130 of the 207 acres of the original San Marino Ranch purchased by Henry E. Huntington in 1903. Today the drive, even on freeways, from Beverley Hills to San Marino seems interminable, but that is no excuse for missing these fascinating gardens.

With limited time one can concentrate on the Desert Garden and the Palm Garden which are both quite close to the Huntington Library building. More than 90 different species of palms grow at Huntington, bordering the pathways and creating elegant avenues; the *Butia* palm with its edible yellow fruit, the European native *Chaemaerops humilis*, the date palm *Phoenix dactylifera* and the Canary Island palm *Phoenix Canariensis*. The thick-trunked Chilean wine palm (*Jubaea chilensis*) and the slender Californian native *Washingtonia filifera*, that so typifies

---

1 Huntington was misspelt as 'Huntingdon' in the original article in *The Age* and has been corrected here.

the streets from Hollywood to Santa Monica, have the appearance of Laurel and Hardy.

The Desert Garden is dramatic in its impact. Its 12 acres contain more than 2500 species – all densely planted. The impression is of a terrestrial coral reef and, ironically, the first specimen noted in the guide is *Euphorbia milii* var. *splendens* – the Crown of Thorns. Other euphorbias include *E. ingens, E. grandicornis* and *E. horrida.*

A fascination of desert plant forms is the likeness they conjure up in the popular imagination. The intriguing specimens carefully nurtured in arid houses in Melbourne or Edinburgh are bigger and better outside at Huntington: Elephant's Foot (*Dioscorea elephantipes*), Bishop's Cap (*Astrophytum myriostigma*), and Living Rock (*Ariocarpus*) and the Golden Barrel Cactus (*Echinocactus Grusonii*), which has a woolly apex and accordian-like ribs that expand or contract according to water storage needs.

The most spectacular part of the Desert Garden is the mammillaria rockery created in 1927 with hundreds of tons of Arizona lava-rock. Some of the largest specimens pre-date the rockery and were brought from Mexico as early as 1912. *Mammillaria compressa* forms mats that creep over rocks creating an unforgettable sight. The snow-white *M. geminispina* is striking amid the red and yellow of other flowering varieties which give color to the rockery between January and June.

Tree forms are also well represented, notably the Blue Palo Verde (*Cercidium floridum*), so characteristic of the arid South Western areas of USA, the desert wattle (*Acacia farnesiana*) and, for those who enjoy 'The Hunting of the Snark', the Boojum Tree (*Idria columnaris*). This curious tree produces tiny leaves from its erect hollow trunk in the rainy season and loses them in the dry season.

Yucca, aloe, agave and crassula enthusiasts will also be well satisfied at Huntington. The only other comparable desert and succulent displays are at Les Cedres in France and Le Jardin Exotique in Monaco.

Like many American botanic gardens, Huntington is a series of specialised gardens and most visitors will appreciate the North Vista created by a broad sweep of lawn leading to an Italian Renaissance fountain with the San Gabriel Mountains in the distance. The perspective is enhanced by 17th century stone statues from Padua. The vista is offset by camellia gardens representative of the main species – *Camellia sasanqua, C. japonica* and *C. reticulata.* A second camellia garden is set close to the Japanese Garden.

It is pleasing to find a section of the Huntington Gardens devoted to Australian flora with over a hundred varieties of eucalyptus. These are well supported by Callistemons, Anigozanthus and Acacias. Across the road there are the subtropical species – cassias, bauhinias, tabebuias and jacarandas. South Africa is represented by leucospermum, gazanias, and the Cape chestnut (*Calodendron capense*).

A superb rose garden, a herb garden, lily ponds, a Shakespeare garden and extensive Japanese gardens complete the specialist areas. The entire park provides an arboretum for tree-lovers.

The self-guiding tour brochures, available at the shop, are clear and informative. But, with the gardens only open between 1 pm and 4.30 pm from Tuesday to Sunday, one visit scarcely taps the pleasures of Huntington.

South Californian weather is notoriously cinematic. Should your visit be marred by rain, do not despair. Take shelter in the Huntington Library or Art Gallery. They hold as many treasures as the gardens.

The Age, 8 February 1985, Weekender, p. 7.

Bogor, a venture in paradise

BOGOR BOTANIC GARDENS, JAVA, INDONESIA. Established: 1817; Area: 275 acres; Highlights: equatorial rainforest, orchid houses, garden walks, bamboos, tropical fruits.

Noble savages, whether Man Friday, Bennelong or Paul and Virginie, fascinated Europeans in the late 18th century. They were believed to lead a Rousseauesque (Jean-Jacques) existence in a Rousseauesque (Henri 'Douanier') landscape of lush growth, perfumed flowers and spicy fruit.

The display of tropical and sub-tropical species in stove house and conservatory, and the planting of rainforest trees in 19th century parks and gardens were botanical spin-offs from this romanticism.

Today a new romanticism inspires the crusade to save pockets of rainforest. Conservatories are again a feature of domestic architecture and botanic gardens are sprucing up their tropical and sub-tropical collections.

Increasing tourism in South-East Asia is introducing Australians to some of the great equatorial gardens including the remarkable Indonesian botanic gardens at Bogor, inland from Jakarta.

Although the gardens were officially opened in 1817, and Stamford Raffles is often, incorrectly, credited with their establishment, it was the Dutch who created the Hortus Bogoriensis in the 18th century.

Like Australia's early botanic gardens, they were located adjacent to a colonial governor's residence, for the village of Bogor was a hill-station where Europeans could escape the enervating heat of Batavia.

The Bibliotheca Bogoriensis in Jalan Raya (the main street) houses a notable array of books illustrating work done by the Dutch botanists. The present town of Bogor is an important centre for research and teaching, with university faculties in agriculture and forestry.

A dominant feature of the Bogor Gardens is the avenue of *Canarium decumanum* (a member of the Burseracae), their trunks swathed in carefully trimmed tropical climbers and their golden excrescence attracting the wild bees. For many years the beeswax was collected for use by the batik craftsmen.

To appreciate a tropical rainforest you need to empty your mind of the horizontal landscape perspective and re-orient, first in the vertical plane, and then to a canopy – the ecological equivalent of a Renaissance ceiling.

The splendor of the epiphytic orchids is breathtaking. There is the queen of orchids (*Grammatophyllum speciosum*) with an inflorescence exceeding six feet and boasting up to 100 flowers; there are the smaller but colorful Dendrobium orchids contrasting with birds' nest ferns (*Asplenium nidus avis*) and staghorn ferns (*Platycerium*).

The orchid houses afford a more comfortable and more comprehensive view of the 5000 orchid varieties in the gardens.

Among the palms at Bogor, a plaque identifies the original oil-nut palm (*Elaeis guineensis*) brought from the west coast of Africa in 1848.

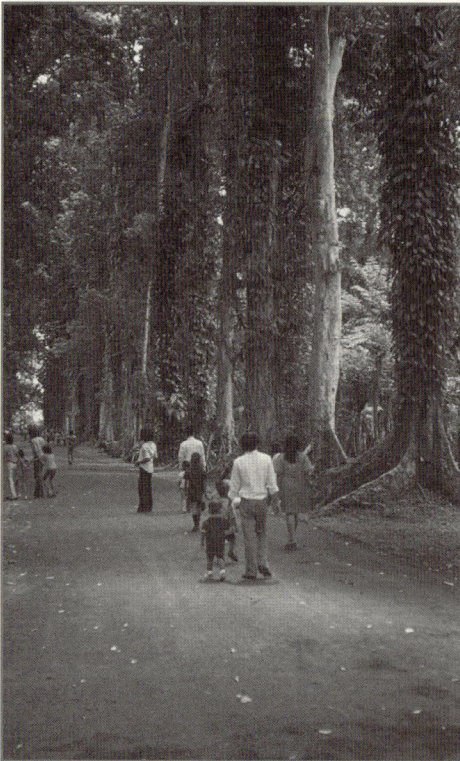

Avenue of Canariums, Bogor Botanic Gardens, Java. Photographer: Eleanor Leigh.

The species readily adapt to Indonesian and Malaysian conditions, contributing much to the regional economy.

Also of commercial importance are the bamboos. *Dendrocalamus*, the giant bamboo, is widely used in Asia for scaffolding and even for reinforcing concrete. *Daemonorops*, Sumatran rattan, is the basic material for much cane furniture.

Some of the fruits seen in Bogor have a Brobdingnagian appearance. The spiky external character of the durian (*Durio zibethinus*) belies the delicacy of its maladorous flesh. The jackfruit (*Artocarpus heterophyllus*), ungainly and shapeless, vies as an oddity with *Phaleria capitata*, which has sweet-scented white flowers covering its trunk like a bubble bath. The flower buds form deep within the tissue of the tree and then burst out through the bark.

Europe's influence is seen in the lawns, the lakes and the paths. The summer residence of the Dutch governor became the Indonesian president's palace, a white colonnaded building reflected in an ornamental pond surrounded by manicured lawn in fine landscape style.

The Queen Astrid Walk passes beds of canna, coleus and crotons displayed in abstract designs. The Lady Raffles walk leads to a small Grecian-style memorial very like the Temple of the Winds in the Melbourne Botanic Gardens.

This raises the question of whether the Bogor Gardens influenced the design of the Melbourne Gardens. William Guilfoyle admits, in his annual report of 1875, that he was 'endeavoring to imitate tropical scenery'.

In his assessment of Guilfoyle's work Professor George Seddon notes the resemblance the Melbourne gardens bear to Bogor. He suggests Guilfoyle was an 'intensely romantic late Victorian' as much as 'a latter-day Capability Brown'.

Few gardens in the world have staff as dedicated as those of Bogor. The standard of cultivation and research has been maintained through the vicissitudes of colonial past, Japanese occupation and the penury imposed by governments with priorities in different directions.

In keeping with contemporary ecological thinking, there is a section of original rainforest set aside for botanic research. Inaccessible to the casual visitor, this is the area of Bogor that my imagination populated with 'noble savages' and even pterodactyls.

The Age, 8 March 1985, Weekender, p. 7.

San Fran fragrance on show

STRYBING ARBORETUM, SAN FRANCISCO. Established: 1937; Area: 71 acres; Highlights: fragrance garden for the blind, redwood trail, native plants, demonstration garden, innovative voluntary support group.

If you go to San Francisco … visit the Strybing Arboretum. Like a jewel in a generous setting, it lies in Golden Gate Park. I suspect that a change in its development was a subconscious response to those who wore flowers in their hair in the late 1960s.

The garden owes its existence to the philanthropy of the 1920s and to the misery of the 1930s. A bequest from Helene Strybing to the City of San Francisco for an arboretum and botanical gardens was furthered by Franklin Roosevelt's New Deal Construction and planting began in 1937 with the assistance of the Workers' Progress Administration program.

The climate of the gardens permits growth of an exceptional range of plants. You can wander along the redwood trail where magnificent Californian redwoods (*Sequoia sempervirens*) grow as they do on the cool moist slopes of the coastal ranges. In a matter of minutes you find yourself in a warmer, drier 'arroyo' landscape where manzanitas, madrones, mahonia, ceanothus and the Californian poppy (*Eschscholzia californica*) are growing.

Elsewhere the famous Californian conifers, *Cupressus macrocarpa*, *Pinus radiata* and the unique *P. torreyana*, represent the vegetation of the southern Californian coast.

Strybing's extremely mild winters allow the tropical Vireya rhododendrons from New Guinea to bloom from November to April, while the fragrant white-flowered Maddenii varieties can be seen from February to April.

The collection of *Rhododendron arboreum* on Heidelberg Hill (so named because it was a beer garden at the 1890s midwinter fair) is of historical significance in the development of modern hybrids.

The original master plan for Strybing envisaged an arboretum similar to Harvard University's Arnold Arboretum in Boston, with geographical and generic groupings of species.

The post-war urban growth of San Francisco led to popular interest in domestic horticulture and in 1959 a second master plan was commissioned. This introduced special interest areas – the redwood trail, the fragrance garden, the demonstration garden, the bird walk, the succulent garden, the garden of Californian native plants and many other small gardens.

Although the area of the arboretum as such was diminished, picturesque spots such as the Jennie Zellerbach garden designed in a semi-circle, and the Anelli garden with its pool, stone lanterns, azaleas and flowering cherries, widened the appeal of Strybing.

Garden of Fragrance in late summer, showing wall built of stones from a Spanish monastery. From the collection of San Francisco Botanical Garden, Helen Crocker Russell Library of Horticulture.

Many public gardens today make provision for the disabled. Strybing Arboretum has a lovely fragrance garden for the visually handicapped. The stone used in the walls of this garden was originally part of a Spanish monastery which William Randolph Hearst planned to reconstruct in Golden Gate Park.

However, the crates in which the stones had been transported were destroyed by fire and the builders lost the construction code painted on the boxes. I am sure the Spanish monks would delight in the present use of their cloisters.

San Franciscans appreciate the practical information and ideas offered in the demonstration garden. This two-acre area was opened in 1965 as a cooperative effort by the arboretum, 'sunset' magazines, nurserymen and other interested individuals. Not only plants but paving, fencing, seating and terrace construction are displayed in a functional setting. Containers for plants in a gamut of materials add variety in texture and form.

Other places have established demonstration gardens. The Edinburgh Gardens have shown hedging plants, noxious weeds and experimental strains of vegetables. Not long ago the Melbourne gardens had a section of lawns, but generally Australia has not taken up the idea.

The thousands of people who visit the annual garden week exhibition suggest that Victorians would welcome a permanent demonstration facility. Perhaps one of the suburban gardens could develop a demonstration garden. What about Footscray or St Kilda or Wattle Park?

Like most contemporary botanic gardens Strybing has a strong voluntary support group. The Strybing Arboretum Society provides a two-year college-accredited course to train volunteer teaching guides who take visitors on general or special interest tours of the gardens. A similar idea here would be a splendid unit for a post-compulsory schooling credit.

The society also organises a gigantic annual plant sale featuring new and unusual plants. Proceeds from this project are used to finance improvements in the gardens.

Often, memorial seats and trees are an aspect of public

gardens. At Strybing there is a practical memorial to Elizabeth Whitney Putnam who 'during a busy life maintained a love for flowers and gardening'. They provided bed-markers and plant-labels.

There is no doubt the flower-power dynamic of San Francisco continues in the ideas that Strybing Arboretum and Botanic Gardens offer to those visiting Golden Gate Park.

The Age, 4 April 1985, pp. 5, 14.

Gardens in touch with the times

NATIONAL BOTANIC GARDENS, CANBERRA. Established: 1950; Area: 40.5 hectares; Highlights: Australian native plants, rainforest gully, nature trail, educational program, publication *Growing Native Plants.*

The redoubtable Walter Burley Griffin envisaged a botanic garden devoted to Australian plants in his original plan for the national capital. Although the first plantings did not occur until 1950, his vision was realised when the Prime Minister of the day, John Gorton, officially opened the National Botanic Gardens in October 1970.

More than 40 hectares on the lower slopes of Black Mountain, with a splendid view over Lake Burley Griffin, provides a distinctive site.

The gardens claim to be primarily a scientific and educational centre, but they do not simply exist for students on school excursions. Rather they recognise the current concept of life-long education and provide a centre for the study of botany and the cultivation of Australian native plants. Specimens collected from all over Australia are propagated in special micro-climates created within the gardens – notably the rainforest gully and the rockery areas. By 1980 there were more than 20,000 species and 3000 genera.

There is no apology for the scientific labelling of plants in the National Botanic Gardens. More than other gardens in Australia, Canberra works to publicise and extend the use of scientific terms. All the literature available to visitors emphasises the importance of correct nomenclature. The plant location guide provides a comprehensively indexed map grid reference and a clear explanation of the system of labelling.

Children can discover things for themselves by following the nature trail which takes them into the upper, more natural section of the area where the study of animal, as well as plant life, is possible. Or they may prefer to go with one of the rangers who will answer their questions. The indoor exhibition and display area always contains examples of children's work relating to plants. It is proof that the education program is returning dividends among the coming generation.

Adults will find a fund of practical information in the series Growing Native Plants published by the National Botanic Gardens. Each volume, 16–24 pages, contains a leading article on horticultural topics and articles on the cultivation of specific native plants. An advisory service is also offered.

The seasonal walks developed by the Sydney and Melbourne gardens are not as appropriate for a native garden. The suggested method of exploration in the Canberra gardens is the marked walk or trail. The Aboriginal trail highlights plants having a particular value to tribal Aborigines; the white arrow walk explores the longer-established section of the gardens on the lower slopes. Better-known Australian varieties such a *Leptospermum* (tea-trees),

The Aboriginal Trail at the National Botanic Gardens, Canberra, in 2008. Photographer: Mark Sheahan.

Melaleuca (paper bark) and *Callistemon* (bottlebrushes)
represent the *Myrtaceae*, while varieties of *Banksia, Grevillea*
and *Hakea* are grouped in the *Proteaceae* area.

From the Acacia section which provides a fine display of
blossom in September, the blue arrow walk winds up Black
Mountain passing a cover of natural Eucalypts. The fascinating
scribbly gums (*Eucalyptus haemastoma* and *E. rossii*) are a
feature. Further up the hillside, areas are set aside for
Prostanthera (mint bush), Papilionaceae (the pea family) and
Rutaceae (boronia and eriostemon).

Both walks end in the rainforest area. In what was once a
dry gully there is now an impressive system of hundreds of fine-
misting sprays controlled by a time-switch, giving a lush, humid
micro-climate suitable for rainforest species, notably ferns.

Complete contrast is provided by the rockery, where huge
embedded slabs of rock provide an environment suitable for
species from Western and Central Australia. Late September and
early October see a brilliant show of color – the startling blue of
Leschenaultia biloba, the softer hues of the *Helichrysum* species,
the red and green of *Anigozanthus manglesii*, the scarlet of
Clianthus formosus.

Quite different again is the marsh garden: habitat for Ajuga,
Lotus and Ranunculus. Future development includes plans for a
tropical glasshouse on the hillside above the rainforest gully.

The Nancy T. Burbidge Amphitheatre is a practical memorial
to a notable botanist. It opened in 1980 and is used as an open-
air classroom or small entertainment area. Its setting, the
Eucalyptus lawn, is a delight.

Recognising contemporary needs, the Canberra Gardens have
a capacious car-park and a small but attractive kiosk, which offers
a variety of national and international dishes. Picnic and barbecue
facilities abound in the neighboring Black Mountain Reserve.

Our national capital provides Australia with a botanic garden
which is doing a fine job for the future. Youngster it may be, but
it is certainly in touch with the times.

The Age, 3 March 1985, Weekender, p. 7.

Let the Brits take you up the garden path ... historically

NYMANS, HANDCROSS, SUSSEX. Established: 1885; Area: 30 acres; Highlights: walled garden, heather garden, rose garden, laurel walk, sunken garden.

The Sussex Weald is a rewarding area for those interested in English gardens. It is easily reached from London and the pleasure of its plants is matched by the delights of cross-country bus trips.

Careful planning of your trip pays dividends. The English Tourist Board produces a touring map 'Visit an English Garden' with gardens arranged under thematic headings – Up The Historical Garden Path; Temples, Topiaries and Tropics; The Green Sleeves of London, and so forth.

The National Trust distributes regional pamphlets describing its gardens. The county booklets of the National Gardens Charitable Trust Scheme give detailed information on all gardens open to visitors be it for one day or all summer. Since 1980 England has adopted the formula used in Scotland where admission fees go to a charity of the owner's choice as well as contributing to the nationally selected charity.

Further useful information comes from the AA Guide, *Stately Homes, Museums, Castles and Gardens in Great Britain* and from the monthly publication, *Out of Town*.

Watch out for dates when a particular village has its gardens open. Fernhurst, Fittleworth, Rogate, Udimore and Winchelsea are Sussex villages that hold annual cooperative open days.

It is advisable to concentrate on one garden or on several in close proximity. You might choose Northiam as a centre and see the Edwin Lutyens–Gertrude Jekyll achievement at Great Dixter

and go on to Coplands, a recently restored and redesigned
garden of one acre.

My recommendation is Handcross for the woodland garden
of The High Beeches and the beauty of Nymans, which will
celebrate its centenary in 1985.

The High Beeches, a 16-acre garden, is notable for its
daffodils, rhododendrons and trees. It was the first of three Sussex
gardens designed by members of the Loder family. The other two
gardens, Leonardslee and Wakehurst Place, are better known.

Nymans is the epitome of a garden cultivated by succeeding
generations. Leonard Messel established it in 1885 and his son,
Colonel L. C. R. Messel, developed it and bequeathed it to the
National Trust in 1954. Since then, his daughter, the Countess of
Rosse, has directed the garden.

Lady Rosse believes gardens, as houses, should reflect the
personalities and aspirations of their makers, mirroring each generation until time and growth mould them into a harmonious whole.

Nymans covers about 30 acres, yet it is intimate and personal.
The walled garden is its heart. This was originally made from an

Nymans: 'At first I thought I was going to be terribly disappointed in the garden but the effect
was rather like increasingly discovering greater pleasure culminating in the dovecote ... The
dovecote was alive with pure white doves and pink climbing roses' (Nina's travel diary, 31
July 1980). Photographer: Nina Crone.

old orchard. The borders were designed with help from William Robinson. Today, in summer, they shimmer with white and mauve *Galegas*, pink, white and mauve *Phlox* and blue and purple *Salvias*.

The Italian fountain, guarded by four globe-shaped yews, is set at the intersection of the borders and the whole garden is backed by a profusion of shrubs: *Aesculus parviflora*, *Clerodendrum trichotomum*, various *Buddleias* and specimen *Magnolias*. It is a happy blend of formal and informal.

After the seclusion of the walled garden, the lawns are breathtaking. The stone gazebo with its dovecote leads the eye to the skeleton of the Great Hall (destroyed by fire in 1947). Here *Magnolia grandiflora* 'Goliath' and a double yellow Banksia rose enhance the old stone. Further along wistaria, winter sweet and clematis vie for attention.

The heather garden at Nymans was one of the first in England. It has hills of flamboyant Irish and Cornish heaths surrounding gnarled trunks of *Erica arborea* and *E. terminalis*. Textural contrast is provided by *Azaleas, Berberis lologensis, Callistemon citrinis* and *Hakea acicularis* while *Embothrium coccineum* and *Sophora microphylla* give a contrast in height.

Misty colors are found in the pergola area where the mauve of wistaria is extended by drifts of *Iris sibirica* around the croquet lawn. Creamy white *Hydrangea arborescens* 'Grandiflora' grow under the pergola.

Old-fashioned roses, which came from Miss Willmott and from French and Italian gardens, surround a wishing-well in the rose garden. Arches, pillars and arbors provide scope for many climbing varieties and the paths are bordered with a deep-blue French form of *Nepeta*.

Australians will notice *Eucryphia cordifolia* and *E. glutinosa*, the original parents of *E. nymansensis*. Other hybrids produced at Nymans include *Magnolia* 'Leonard Messel' (*M. Kobus* x *M. stellata*) and *Camellia* 'Leonard Messel' (*C. Williams* var. *Mary Christian* x *C. reticulata* var. *Captain Rawes*).

Lady Rosse is unstinting in her praise of the gardeners who

developed Nymans. James Comber, who gathered plants in Tasmania in the 1920s, and Cecil Nice each worked there for well over 50 years.

Altogether Nymans is a fine horticultural gallery and a joy to those in search of the English garden.

The Age, 24 May 1985, Weekender, p. 9.

Edinburgh's plants were reared for their medicinal value

ROYAL BOTANIC GARDENS, EDINBURGH, SCOTLAND. Established: 1670; Area: 50 acres (at Inverleith); Highlights: heather garden, rock garden, peat garden, rhododendron walk, exhibition plant houses, botanical research.

Twice in their history, the Royal Botanic Gardens of Edinburgh have been moved. They were first established in 1670 near Holyrood Palace. A hundred years later the entire plant collection was transferred to a new site on the main Leith Road; and in 1820 the contents of that garden were replanted on the present site at Inverleith.

Accustomed to well-established and carefully maintained botanic gardens, it is easy for us to think they exist solely for our pleasure. Yet plant research has been the primary concern of the world's greatest botanic gardens.

The Holyrood gardens were supervised by a doctor and their purpose was to grow medicinal plants for Edinburgh University. A botanist was appointed after an additional garden, attached to Trinity Hospital, was acquired. (The hospital site is where Waverly station now stands.)

Three hundred years ago, research at Edinburgh centred on

herbal and medical knowledge. More recently it has concentrated on taxonomy – the identification and classification of plants – and has become authoritative on rhododendrons and primulas as a result of George Forrest's plant-collecting expeditions. Current research involves *Ericaceae* (the heaths), *Gesneriaceae* (African violets) and *Zingiberaceae* (the ginger family). The public rarely appreciates the vast stock of plants grown behind the scenes as material for research.

The Royal Botanic Gardens are at their peak during the Edinburgh Festival and thus most overseas visitors see them in summer.

Entry from the east gate on Inverleith Row brings you appropriately to the heather garden. Thirty varieties of Scottish heather flower between June and October. Popular low-growing forms include the bell heather (*Erica cinerea*) and a winter heather (*E. herbacea*). The tree heather or French *bruyère* (*E. arborea*) is interesting as its roots are used to make 'briar' pipes. The variety in Edinburgh (*E. arborea* var. *alpina*) is a hardy one, although it reaches only two and a half metres in height.

The rock garden, established last century, has been completely rebuilt with rock from Ben Ledi and sandstone from Dumfries. Prostrate conifers, junipers, cotoneasters and dwarf rhododendrons (*R. forrestii* var. *repens* and *R. lapponicum*) give ground cover while gentians, saxifrages, campanulas, pulsatillas, penstemons and primulas provide pockets of interest and color.

For contrast one can visit the shaded, moist peat garden where *shortias* and *phyllodoces* flourish. Primulas and trilliums greet the spring followed by ourisias (native to Tasmania), *Meconopsis villosa* and *M. chelidonifolia*.

In May and June, a stroll can be enjoyed in the arboretum to admire the birches – *Betula ermanii* from Asia, a *B. papyrifera*, the canoe birch, from North America, and *B. jacquemonti* from the Himalayas – followed by the rhododendron walk up the hill to Inverleith House. *Rhododendron campanulata, R. dichroanthum* and *R. lacteum* blend together in gorgeous show.

Inverleith House, used for exhibitions and special functions, is as gracious as its surroundings are beautiful. Nearby, the tea room – definitely not a kiosk – offers sweet, sticky buns and tea.

During a summer excursion to the gardens you tend to discount the rigors of the Scottish winter but even in that bitter season the Edinburgh gardens have much to offer. The exhibition plant houses are considered world leaders. Opened in 1967, they are so spacious that an illusion of landscape is possible.

The specimens in the cactus and succulent house range from the tiny Lithops (the 'Living Stones'), to the giant Euphorbias and Echinocercus. The warm temperate aquatic house holds the sensuous night-flowering cacti *Selenicereus* and *Hylocereus*, while Australians can delight in finding wattle, bottlebrush and kangaroo paw in the temperate plant house.

Highlights of the tropical aquatic house include the spectacular *Victoria amazonica*, the Egyptian paper-reed (*Cyperus papyrus*), rice (*Oryza sativa*) and the traveller's tree (*Ravenala madagascariensis*). Further plant houses are devoted to ferns, cycads and orchids.

The most interesting tree in the temperate palm house is *Livistona australis*, whose name commemorates the Laird of Livingstone. He gave many of his plants to the first botanic gardens at Holyrood. Two specimens in the 150-year-old tropical palm house should be sought out – the Talipot palm (*Corypha umbraculifera*) from India which produces a huge inflorescence up to 10 metres long, with millions of individual flowers and *Sabal blackburniana*, the West Indian fan palm, reputed to be 160 years old.

The alpine house is designed to maintain a constant, cool, room temperature for the tender species. This is done by overlapping the display staging with a deep layer of moist sand into which the pots are set.

Of the botanic gardens in Britain, only Oxford is older than Edinburgh. After two moves and with three outstations established – near Dunoon, Stranraer and Peebles – it seems that the Royal Botanic Gardens in Edinburgh were meant to stay at Inverleith.

The Age, 28 June 1985, Weekender, p. 7.

Cornwall's 'Farm of the Spring' was built on the proceeds of slavery

TRENGWAINTON, NEAR PENZANCE, CORNWALL. Established: 1692; Area: 98 hectares; Highlights: rhododendron collection, magnolia collection, series of walled gardens, stream garden, commemorative trees.

The essence of summer in Cornwall is, for me, walking down country lanes between dry stone walls overgrown with field flowers. On a recent stay there, my destinations were as varied as the delights: morning sunshine along the cliff paths from Mousehole to glittering Lamorna Cove, inland to St Buryan's for a ploughman's lunch, past the standing stones called 'the merry maidens', across meadows, over stiles, through farmyards to Madron, and, in the late afternoon to Trengwainton.

The name in Cornish means the Farm of the Spring and a dwelling has been there from the 17th century. Today the property, of 98 hectares, belongs to the National Trust. Near Penzance, it faces due south, overlooking Mount's Bay, St Michael's Mount and The Lizard. This meridianal aspect is ideal for frost-tender plants and Trengwainton is notable for exotic species.

Sir Rose Price, who bought the estate in 1814, was the first to show interest in the garden. This son of a wealthy Jamaican sugar planter surrounded the house with trees and lined the drive with ash, beech and sycamore. He also built the remarkable series of walled gardens and raised terrace beds.

Unhappily, the family fortune was destroyed by the economic collapse of plantations and slave-owners following Wilberforce's *Emancipation Act*. Trengwainton was sold, eventually settling with the Bolitho family in the second half of the 19th century.

Lieutenant-Colonel Edward Bolitho, who inherited

Trengwainton in 1925, began creating a new garden. With G. H. Johnstone of Trewithen and Lawrence Johnston of Hidcote, he took a share in Kingdon Ward's 1927 plant-collecting expedition to Assam and Burma. Trengwainton's impressive rhododendron collection is founded on seed gathered on that journey. Young shrubs were nurtured in the walled gardens and later planted behind Price's shelter belts.

The only rhododendrons of earlier date (apart from the thickets of *Rhododendron ponticum* near the house), were *R. falconeri* planted in the 1850s and *R. griffithianum* planted in 1904. During the 1930s careful propagation introduced *R. macabeanum, R. elliottia, R. taggianum* and *R. concateans* to Britain.

R. cv '*Morvah*' and *R.* cv '*Johnnie Johnson*' were both raised at Trengwainton. They are a tribute to the hybridising skill of G. W. Thomas, head gardener from 1924 until 1947. Other worthwhile specimens include the magenta-flowered *R. obtusum* cv *Amoenum*, the pure white fragrant *R. mucronatum*, the red *R.* cv '*Elizabeth*', the yellow *R. campylo-carpum* and the sweet-scented *R. maddenii*.

Late afternoon sunshine sheds a golden glow over the walls of the kitchen garden. (As this is not open to the public, you need to make a special request to see it.) It is a secret, bountiful place. Beds are sloped towards southern warmth, and the espaliered fruit-trees are as decorative as they are productive. Gooseberries, black currants, raspberries and strawberries grow in profusion, holding promise of jams and jellies; carrots,

'Glittering' Lamorna Cove near Penzance. 'After reaching Penzance, immediately took the bus to Madron to visit Trengwainton Gardens – not the ideal time as the gardens are spring gardens' (Nina's travel diary, 12 July 1980). Photographer: Nina Crone.

beetroot, asparagus, lettuce, parsley and chives are ready for picnics in the meadow or tea on the top lawn.

Also worth noting are the stream garden and the trees in the meadow – *Quercus robur* planted to commemorate Queen Victoria's diamond jubilee in 1897: a *Tilia* species marking Edward VII's coronation; the Bhutan Pine (*Pinus wallichiana*), planted by the Queen Mother in 1962 and the Mexican Pine (*Pinus patula*), planted by Princess Anne 10 years later.

The following April, I revisited Trengwainton for the magnolias. A superb specimen near the gate greeted me. It dated back to 1936 and was a fast-growing hybrid of *Magnolia campbellii* and *M. heptapeta* raised by the celebrated Mr Veitch of Exeter.

Other interesting hybrids are *M.* x *high-downensis* (*M. sinensis* x *M. wilsonii*) which was first grown at Highdown in Sussex from seedlings raised at Caerhays in Cornwall. It blooms in early June, producing pure white pendant flowers. There is also *M.* cv '*Charles Raffill*', an intersubgeneric hybrid of *M. campbellii* and *M. mollicomata*, with pink flowers.

Magnolias from many countries find a place at Trengwainton. An early arrival (1926) was *M. campbellii* from Sikkim. From Tibet came *M. globosa*, distinguished by the down on the underside of its broad leaves, and the creamy-flowered and broad-leaved *M. rostrata*. The fragrant *M.* x *watsonii* is of Japanese origin while Chinese species include *M. cylindrica*, *M. delavayi* and *M. sargentiana* var. *robusta*.

Nor are the well-loved favorites neglected. *M. sprengeri* cv '*Diva*' was planted in 1958 and there is *M. campbellii* cv '*Lanarth*' with its large cyclamen-colored flowers contrasting with the white daintiness of *M. stellata*.

The happy coincidence of Kingdon Ward's expedition, Colonel Edward Bolitho's inheritance and a generation of skilled Cornish gardeners makes Trengwainton a remarkable repository of Asian flora in England and a marvellous place to visit in the northern spring or summer.

The Age, 2 August 1985, Weekender, p. 7.

Behind many a great man is a great gardener

Mt Vernon, Virginia; garden of George Washington. Cooks' Cottage, Melbourne; garden of Captain Cook.

In times past 'front garden' and 'back garden' were as much signals of status as 'upstairs' and 'downstairs'. George Washington had a magnificent front garden; he was a general, and President of the United States. James Cook senior had a useful back garden; he was a Yorkshire stonemason.

In 1759 George Washington was establishing his plantation home, Mount Vernon, in Virginia. The same year the British Admiralty commended Captain James Cook for survey work in Newfoundland waters. Cook had little time between voyages to visit the cottage his parents had built at Great Ayton in Yorkshire.

Like all planters, Washington was a prolific correspondent. From London he ordered Batty Langley's *New Principles of Gardening*; from Germany he sought 'a compleat kitchen gardener with a competent knowledge of flowers'. He penned letters of thanks 'for Acorns, Nutts and seed of trees or plants not common in this country', and letters of instruction: 'tell the Gardener, when he dresses the Artichokes, to put up a number of Slips for a Gentleman of my acquaintance in Philadelphia'.

Such recorded detail of life at Mount Vernon made restoration of this garden a much easier task than was the reconstruction of an 18th century Yorkshire garden around Cooks' Cottage, re-erected in Melbourne's Fitzroy Gardens.

Professor Carrick Chambers of the University of Melbourne's School of Botany, who carried out the research for the Melbourne project, deplored the lack of documented evidence of

18th century cottage garden design. He was obliged to use a mid-19th century account of Cooks' Cottage. This mentioned only five species – ivy, lilac, sycamore, crabapple and hawthorn. Nonetheless, a delightful cottage garden has been reconstructed – 'with some poetic licence' insists Professor Chambers.

The approach to Mount Vernon is from the west where the bowling green, a fiddle-shaped lawn, is bordered by serpentine avenues. These shady carriage drives sweep up to the circular 'courtyard' lawn in front of the house. They are flanked by shrubberies which screen the formal gardens.

No carriage drive for the Cooks; their cottage stood hard on the roadway. No front garden – only English ivy softening the brick building.

It seems that James Cook senior had little interest in his garden. The reconstructed one is about one-third longer than the Great Ayton original. The reasons are soundly practical – inclusion of a lime-tree, already growing nearby; a more appropriate position for the mill-race, and better access for visitors.

Where Washington was concerned with garden design, the cottage was concerned with productivity. Cook had one bed for fruit and vegetables – celeriac, leeks, onions, shallots and berry fruit. Red and black currants were useful for puddings, jams and jellies. Gooseberries were the subject of much competition in the villages; a horticultural catalogue of 1780 listed 320 varieties.

Washington had a large kitchen garden with espaliered fruit-trees and vegetables in beds of geometric design. Each week his gardener submitted a written report. These reports still exist. They mention asparagus, beans, beets, carrots, cauliflower, cucumbers, eggplant, lettuce, okra, parsnips, peas, peppers, potatoes, radish, rhubarb, spinach, squash, tomatoes and turnips. For fruit, Washington grew apples, apricots, Morello cherries, figs, grapes, lemons, limes, nectarines, oranges, peaches, pears and damson plums.

The hedgerows around Cooks' Cottage provided nuts, berries, leaves for salads, flowers for flavoring and, in winter, fuel. Beneath them grew wild strawberries, bluebells and harebells.

Visitors to Mt Vernon often brought plants for their host. Friends from Massachusetts brought spruce and hemlock; the French botanist, André Michaux, brought an evergreen species of Rhamnus and a kinsman from South Carolina supplied a live oak, a palmetto and southern magnolias. From a gift of English boxwood, Washington's gardeners propagated enough material to edge the paths and plant the intricate parterres.

The general's pride was a small botanic garden of exotic plants, among them material from China and from the Philadelphian naturalist-nurseryman, William Bartram.

No room for such indulgence in the Cooks' garden but it is a delightful place on a sunny summer afternoon. The bees buzz about the lavender border and behind it grow angelica, fennel, parsley, land cress (the watercress is found in the millrace), salad burnet, tarragon and carraway. The crescent garden is bright with English marigolds and pretty with pink, purple and white candytuft. A characteristic cottage garden effect is developing as self-sown heartsease invades the other beds. Roses, laburnum, honeysuckle, lily-of-the-valley, lilac and honesty combine in the mixed bed to evoke a strong feeling of England. The plants are representative species and varieties which could have been found in a cottage garden in Great Ayton in the mid-18th century.

One of Washington's overseas visitors recorded: 'The General has never left America but when one sees this house and garden, it seems as if he copied the best of the grand old homesteads of England.' Faithful restoration enables today's visitors to make their own judgment.

But Jack is as good as his master and it is fitting that we can also see the reconstructed cottage garden of a humble Yorkshire stonemason.

The Age, 13 September 1985, Weekender, p. 7.

A garden's role in the flowering of peace and understanding

Today is World Peace Day within the International Year of Peace. Much has been made of the 'Peace' rose and the amazing series of coincidences that lay behind its development in war-torn Europe and its presentation to the United Nations delegates at the 1945 San Francisco Conference.

Antonia Ridge's book *For Love of a Rose* is a timely reprint by Faber. It tells the story of 'Peace', the Meilland rose, and makes good reading for Peace Year.

Although we may pass commemorative statues and explanatory plaques with unseeing eyes and insensitive minds, gardens often have expressed hope for the future or have remembered the ideals espoused in the past.

A most extensive peace garden is situated on the United States–Canadian border where North Dakota meets Manitoba, almost due north of Bismarck. It was established in 1932 with a vow that 'We two nations dedicate this garden and pledge ourselves that as long as we shall live we will not take up arms against one another.'

The 931 hectare park is used for international camping programs, for athletics, hiking, music and cultural activities. As well, a formal landscaped area is set aside for 'gardening arts'.

In Hiroshima, the Peace Park marks the epicentre of the atomic explosion which devastated the city in August 1945. The park is relatively unadorned and limited in area, but the message, carved in the stone cenotaph, is significant: 'Rest in peace for the mistake will not be repeated.' Nagasaki, the other city which suffered atomic attack, has a large Peace Park laid out in a setting of woods, ponds and river.

Admirable as such parks are, I prefer gardens with plantings given in friendship from one country to another to all the commemorative or admonitory statues.

Jell's Park, Glen Waverley, has a grove of *Prunus* 'Shirofugen' presented to Victoria by the Prime Minister of Japan in 1980. As these trees grow we will be able to go cherry-blossom viewing and appreciate a custom that is part of the Japanese way of life.

In New South Wales, the Cowra Tourist and Development Corporation has established a garden in classical Japanese style. This furthers the goodwill and understanding engendered when compassionate citizens of Cowra tended the graves of the Japanese who died in the prisoner-of-war outbreak in 1944.

Ken Nakajima designed the Cowra garden with assistance from the School of Environmental Design at the Canberra College of Advanced Education. He incorporated features of the notable 17th century stroll garden at the Shugakuin Imperial Villa in Kyoto into his plan, which fits comfortably into the Australian landscape.

The Cowra garden unfolds its delights in a measured fashion – gently at first, then with quickening pace and more dramatic features.

Initially the visitor meanders over the lower slopes admiring plantings of *Viburnum tomentosum, Acer palmatum* and *Crytomeria japonica.* A small post bears the inscription 'May Peace Prevail on Earth!'

The path then swings across the hill. It is bordered on one side by *Photinia glabra rubra, Euonymus aureo-marginatus* and *Azalea indica.* These are massed and trimmed to sculptured perfection, suggesting a billowing tapestried hedge.

My visit to Cowra was in March, when drifts of blue and white petunias edged the other side of the path with subdued color. In a Japanese garden, color from flowers is carefully limited to maintain a dominance of greenery.

The view from the succeeding upward traverse is totally

unexpected – a lake and a teahouse situated on an island in it. (The tapestried hedge disguises the retaining wall of the lake.) In all a fine replica, on a much smaller scale, of Shugakuin.

In March, color here comes from yellow *Lantana camara* and pompom chrysanthemums. The still water mirrors an artfully positioned stone lantern. The strong horizontal dimension gives a remarkable sensation of space, light and peace.

Beyond the lake, the mood changes. The dimension is vertical, the path steeper. Rocky outcrops threaten. The stream is turbulent, rapids and waterfall assert themselves. The greenery is sombre ivy. Trees are trimmed to emphasise the trunks and minimise foliage.

Subtle color derives from the pink, white and mauve blossom of *Lagerstroemia indica* in March. It suggests mist wafting off into the 'borrowed scenery' of the Australian landscape – *Eucalyptus melliodora*, a stray peppercorn (*Schinus molle*) and the bleached grass and sky.

The summit brings patches of grass flecked with daisies, and a bird's-eye view of the entire garden and its beauty.

May gardens always be planted to dispel the seeds of war. Let us understand the gardens that other people plant. The making of a garden is a peaceful and productive endeavor.

The Age, 16 September 1986, p. 27.

Fashion of the Tudors finds modern favor

In answer to a reader's query, 'What is a knot garden?'
ALISON DALRYMPLE examines a style that is back in vogue.

Time and again in England's history, eras of peace and prosperity have brought innovation in garden styles.

The Tudor knot garden appeared after the Wars of the Roses, the 'landscape' gardens of 'Capability' Brown amid the mercantilist expansion of the 18th century, and the 'Surrey' gardens of Gertrude Jekyll in the peace and plenty of the Edwardian period. Each style gave great pleasure, in the making and in the beholding.

A new Latin grammar book, published in 1519 for Eton and Winchester scholars, relates how 'the knotte garden serveth for pleasure, the potte garden for profitte', and adds 'Let us walk into the knotte garden'.

As it developed in Tudor times, the knot garden was a small square or rectangular plot where a pattern of interlacing ribbon design – the more intricate the better – was picked out in low, dense-growing plants.

If flowers filled the intervening spaces solidly it was a 'closed knot' but if paths of grass, sand or brick led through the garden beds it was an 'open knot'.

Ribbon designs were a common motif in Tudor and Stuart decorative work – in embroidery, interior design and architecture. Inspiration may have come from Celtic designs, Islamic decoration or Flemish strapwork.

Agricultural and horticultural writers of the time devoted much space to the planning of knot gardens '… which may be set either with thyme of Issope at the discretion of the gardener'.

Another authority urged simplicity and good proportion, recommending close-growing evergreens – lavender, rosemary, germander, thyme and box – with interlacing threads of different herbs to provide contrast and emphasise the 'overs and unders'.

The plants were kept shorn and the fragrant clippings provided strewing material for floors and freshening for closets. The scent from the knot gardens was commonly thought useful in combating pestilential air, thus preserving a healthy atmosphere.

Violets, cowslips, primroses, pansies, pinks and wallflowers filled the knots and gave seasonal color at Hampton Court, where Wolsey made 'knottes so enknotted it cannot be exprest'.

Francis Bacon scorned such 'toys' claiming in his essay 'On Gardens' that one might '... see as good sights many times in tarts'. Documentary evidence from his time suggests that the knot garden fascinated his contemporaries.

Estate account books of the period record payments '... for diligence in making knottes', or '... for the setting of herbs and clipping of knottes'.

Sir Thomas Hanmer, who retired to his house at Bettisfield in Flintshire during Cromwell's regime, wrote in considerable detail

of the plants set in his 'four little bordered beds in the midst of the bordered knot'.

There were '… seven ranks of 26 distinct kinds of tulips, colchicums and anemones … crown imperials, six rows of iris, polyanthuses, daffodils … hyacinths, jonquils, narcissus and black and grey fritillaries'.

John Parkinson argued the advantages and disadvantages of using herbs for garden knots in Jacobean times. He advocated the newer fashion of 'dead materials' such as pebbles and the shank bones of sheep, '… well cleansed and boyled, stuck in the ground small end downwards and knuckle head upwards [to] prettily grace out the ground'. However, he did consider the European use of jaw bones 'too gross'.

Eventually the small, planted knot garden gave way to the elaborate and extensive parterre, where brick chips, chalk, gravels and coal dust highlighted the designs that surrounded stately homes or French châteaux.

Some notable knot gardens are maintained in England – at Hampton Court, Hatfield House and New Place in Stratford. Tudor House in Southampton has a knot derived from the French classic on the subject of 'L'agriculture et la maison rustique', and the National Trust has undertaken two splendid reconstructions of open knots at Moseley Old Hall in Staffordshire and Little Moreton Hall in Cheshire.

In America, there are examples of knot gardens in the Brooklyn Botanic Gardens, New York, at the National Herb Garden in Washington, DC, and at Filoli outside San Francisco.

The knot garden today is finding renewed favor for practical reasons of space and labor as much as for its use of herbs and fragrance plants.

The Age, 16 June 1987, p. 27.

Extract from Nina's travel diary

9 June 1960:

[At Hampton Court] '[T]he walled gardens – first a breath-taking riot of colour enchanted as a painter's palette that settles into a formal design of red and green in the equally charming Knot Garden.

Heatwave evokes memories of Athens' cooler corners

The eight-day heatwave that scorched Greece last week revived memories for ALISON DALRYMPLE of heatwaves passed in the classic, but crowded, city of Athens.

Heatwaves in any city are unpleasant, but in a place like Athens with few gardens and little greenery they are a formidable experience.

Athens stretches away from the Acropolis, covering the outlying hills with concrete apartment blocks and offices. There are relatively few tree-lined boulevards, grassy squares or parks as we know them.

The open spaces of Lycabettus and Philopappas are a bleached and faded green. The citrus stands in the National Gardens near Syntagma Square are lost in the shimmering mirage or the veil of pollution.

The single thread of the commuter railway, now buckling in midsummer heat, leads to verdant Kifissia, the garden suburb of Athens. Last Easter Monday the temperature and the glare from sun-scorched concrete led me to take this train. It rattled through a canyon of flats where an occasional persistent climbing rose attained a remarkable height or a geranium-filled window-box cheered an otherwise depressing wall.

Kifissia refreshed mind and body, with its villas revelling in lush gardens, its leafy streets, its busy thoroughfares bright with flower-stalls and full of all the promises held in seedsmen's shops. On the return trip to town, everyone was carrying bunches of lilac.

In the heat, Athenians also seek relief in the city's public gardens. The Zapplo Gardens and the National Gardens have very little open space. The dominant features are the shady arcades where gravel paths wind between beds of orange trees (*Citrus aurantium* and *C. vulgaris*), pines and cypress.

For the visitor from Australia there is a formality altogether different from home, and yet there are surprising pleasures – the huge square pergola covered with mauve wistaria which makes a sweet-scented and shady canopy for seats beneath, or the nearby belvedere which gives a breathtaking, bird's-eye view of the pergola, looking like a ruffled purple sea.

Feral cats abound in the gardens. In spite of admonitory notices, Athenians keep releasing unwanted animals there. In April I found one golden creature sunbathing among the poppies and creamy stocks. Today I wonder whether that hedonistic beast has survived the blistering summer.

A small botanic museum also offers relief from the sun. There are no souvenir counters, no information brochures, no staff on duty. The displays have been lovingly mounted with that sense of proportion inherent in Greek architecture and art. One shows the history of the gardens (originally the Royal Gardens of Queen Amalia), another the infinite variety of seeds and seed-cases, a third a range of garden tools.

As I retraced my steps to Syntagma Square, the gardeners were hard at work dyking the beds of trees. As there are few sprinkler systems in the gardens in April, irrigation channels or hoses were carefully controlling the use of water. I cannot picture how the gardeners are coping in heatwave conditions.

The Evzone guards are always on duty at the Tomb of the Unknown Warrior on Syntagma Square. Around the corner you will find the flower shops of Athens. They provide a glorious pool of color as yellow and red tulips vie for attention with wine-red stocks, fragrant lilac, snowy viburnum and pink roses.

Beyond Piraeus, in the heat haze, are

Clemenceau ('Clem') – Nina's beloved, hedonistic feline. Photographer: Nina Crone.

the islands – Poros, Aegina and Hydra, often short of water yet
bright with cyclamen splashes of giant pig-face and swathes of
vivid bougainvillea.

Above all, however, the wildflowers of Greece impress the
visitor. The ever-present scarlet of the spring poppy (*Papaver
rhoeas*) with its black core, the dainty summer *Dianthus biflorus*,
the flower of Zeus, and the golden *Sternbergia sicula* of autumn.

If you deplore the lack of gardens and greenery in Athens,
remember the gods have blessed the slopes of Mount Parnassus,
the groves of Olympia, the plain of Marathon and the islands of
the Aegean Sea with incomparable wildflowers. In heatwaves
they are the great survivors.

The Age, 4 August 1987, p. 27.

Gardens in Leningrad, USSR

Not only in this fortieth anniversary year of victory in the
Great Patriotic War (the Second World War, to us), but
always, Leningraders want visitors to see Piskarevskoye.

Here, almost half a million nameless heroes lie in common
graves. The burial mounds stretch in rows for nearly a kilometre.
Each has a concrete marker … 1941 … 1942 … 1943 … A star
indicates the soldiers, oak-leaves the civilians.

I saw Piskarevskoye in April when the scene is saddest. The
thawing snow is dirty-grey, puddles abound, the trees are still
leafless and sombre wooden covers protect the roses that will
blossom blood-red for summer. The solemn notes of
Shostakovich's 'Leningrad' Symphony override the stillness. A

single yellow tulip lies in isolation on a memorial stone. Where, I wondered, in all snow-bound Leningrad, did someone find this brave bloom?

Several days later, I passed a rough-cast wall. Set into this were large display windows bright with *Primula obconica*, *Cineraria* species and all manner of greenhouse finery. My taxi-driver referred to this place in English as 'The House of Flowers'.

On the corner stood the conservatory packed with unseasonal colour. Behind this I found the hot-houses which forced the early tulips placed on the graves at Piskarevskoye.

Other tulips brighten Leningrad in spring but you have to wait until late May or early June to see them. I saw two thousand planted on the Spit of Vasilievsky Island as a token of respect and friendship from the people of Rotterdam to the people of Leningrad.

You also find tulips edging the paths of Letny Sad, the Summer Garden, established 250 years ago by Peter the Great. Eighteenth century marble statues beneath oaks, limes and elms make it one of the world's most elegant gardens. The fine proportions and delicate design of the railings and gates on Nab Kutuzova are enhanced by glimpses of the Neva and the bordering Fontanka, Moika and Swan canals.

From December to April, the garden is snow-covered and the statues are protected by wooden boxes which look like the classic Australian outhouse.

Letny Sad is complemented by two adjacent gardens – the Mikhailovsky Garden and the Field of Mars, a 25-acre park originally known as the Tsarina's Meadow.

From 8 September 1941 until 18 January 1943, Leningrad was bitterly besieged and doggedly

Gates of the Summer Garden in the greyness of Leningrad in April. Photographer: Nina Crone.

defended. As the surrounding troops tightened their stranglehold Leningraders saw the magnificent palaces and gardens of Peterhof and Pushkin devastated. At Pavlovsk, the invaders cut down 70,000 trees.

Happily, these estates have been painstakingly and faithfully restored so that fountains and statues, canals and conceits, palaces and parterres thrill the thousands of summer visitors.

After the siege, Leningrad established 'The Green Belt of Glory' to mark the line of defence around the city. To the north there are two notable parks. The Kirov Park, on Yelagin Island, was laid out in 1932 and has been planted with 18,000 trees to create natural parkland. It is home of the White Nights festivities each June.

Four hundred and fifty acres on neighbouring Krestovsky Island make up the Primorsky Victory Park with its theatres, exhibition halls, bathing and boating facilities.

In the south-west, close to the giant Kirov engineering works, a lane of 900 birch trees marks the former front line of defence and recalls the total number of blockade days.

To the south of the city is Moscow Victory Park with its avenues and flowerbeds, and further on, the 'green glory' of Pulkovo Heights. Here, more mass graves match those of Piskarevskoye in the eastern section of the green belt.

The famous 'road of life', which brought supplies from Finland by way of frozen Lake Ladoga, is commemorated by a 15-metre-high flower of marble and concrete. It bears an inscription in a child's hand: 'Let there always be sunshine.'

In a latitude approaching the Arctic Circle (Leningrad is

Extract from Nina's travel diary

11 April 1985:

As there were two hours before we set off for Rayliv I decided to visit some of the botanic sites of Leningrad and organised a taxi to go to the Summer Garden, the House of Flowers and the Botanic Gardens. At that hour of the day all three were closed – perhaps as well since I only just had time to locate them and take what snaps I was able.

60° N), there is little enough sunshine for growth. In the parks, nature is supplemented by man's artistic and engineering output – fountains, statues, monuments – which can withstand five months of snow and ice.

Nevertheless the city has a respected botanical tradition. Medicinal plants were cultivated on Apothecary's Island from 1713 and a century later the area became the St Petersburg Botanical Gardens. The Komarov Botanical Institute was set up in 1931 and quickly became a major research centre. The war-time blockade destroyed the plant houses, but today the plant collection contains over 10,000 species. Of these, 4500 are tropical or sub-tropical. They are nurtured in the re-built glasshouses and the associated Botanical Museum has one of the finest herbaria in Europe.

Olga Berggolts, a broadcaster during the siege of Leningrad, composed the promise enshrined at Piskarevskoye, 'None is forgotten, nothing is forgotten'. This is true. Even the parks remember.

Previously unpublished

Tashkent, Uzbekistan, USSR

A fter the soft grey smudginess of snow-bound Leningrad, the sunshine and colour of Tashkent in April was brilliant and hard-edged. The airport car-park was bright with the deep pink blossom of the Judas tree (*Cercis siliguastrum*), one of my favourite trees.

Tashkent is one of the greenest cities in the Soviet Union. Almost every street is edged by trees – Lombardy or Asiatic poplars, plane trees, acacias, chestnuts, lime trees, oaks or maples. Throughout its 2000-year history the city has been watered by the Chirchuk River which springs from the snows of the Tian Shan Mountains. The famous tree-lined alleys, known locally as *arils* or *aryks*, are found along the banks of the Anchor and Salar Canals. They provide much-appreciated pockets of coolness in a city which experiences exceptionally hot summers.

Strolling south from Lenin Square, along the Anchor Canal, you reach Yuri Gagarin Park. In spite of its modern name, this area was established before the Russian Revolution by a provincial governor who enjoyed gardens. He imported rare species from Moscow and from the celebrated Nikitsky Gardens on the Crimean Peninsula.

After the Revolution, the total area of eight hectares was turned into a botanic garden whose work centred on the acclimatisation of species new to Central Asia and on the cultivation of native roses. By the late 1940s, the garden was far too small for scientific research and it became a people's park.

The largest park in Tashkent is the 70-hectare Leninist Komsomol Park with its big lake. It too has an interesting genealogy. Originally the site of the Beshagach Gate on the caravan route to Kokand Khanate, it became a quarry and a brickworks in 1870, after the demolition of the old city wall. Following the closure of the brickworks, the Komsomols (teenage communist youth groups) built a reservoir in the old quarry in 1939.

Thousands of trees and shrubs were planted around the reservoir, the first in Tashkent, and as further water storages were constructed, the Komsomol Park became recreational with the introduction of amusement centres, boating facilities and a children's miniature railway.

The botanical gardens of the Uzbek Academy of Sciences are well worth a visit if you are able to arrange it. This is not always easy unless you are with a special interest group or unless you have several days in the city so that you can be quietly insistent with your Intourist guide.

'I want to see the botanical gardens, please.
– They are closed.
– At three o'clock in the afternoon?
– To-day.
– Then we'll go to-morrow. At 11.30!'

The gardens are situated in the north-east suburban area of Tashkent, on the bank of the Salar Canal. They were planned and developed during the 1950s as a place for popular instruction as well as for scientific research.

Various plant environments have been created so that visitors experience a coniferous forest where larch, juniper and pines give an impression of the Byelorussian landscape which is so different from the steppes of Central Asia.

A birch grove allows you to appreciate the numerous species of this genus – broad-leaved birches, silver birches, golden birches, black birches, paper birches, canoe birches and many more.

> ## *Extract from a letter*
>
> **To Tommy Garnett, editor of the Gardening section of *The Age*, 3 March 1985:**
>
> *… I leave on 2ⁿᵈ April for a fortnight in the USSR. Rather an unexpected assignment to a country I never had any great desire to visit. I do hope I'll be able to see some of the gardens if the time schedule permits.*

Surprisingly there is a simulated American prairie which leads into a section displaying maple trees and Manchurian walnuts. These in their turn shelter a comprehensive collection of dog roses. Even semi-tropical vines and lianas have been inveigled into winding their way over barberry bushes to give an impression of a jungle. It is all rather like a botanical Disneyland!

These botanical gardens played a key role in encouraging the public planting of street trees in Tashkent. They gave municipal gardeners a wide assortment of plants exotic to Uzbekistan but now commonplace in the capital city – the pyramidal oak, the tulip poplar, and the Japanese quince. Spruce and arborvitae line Lenin Square and Lenin Avenue. Chestnuts, liquidambars, red cedars, and Crimean pines were acclimatised.

New varieties of roses, tulips and irises were developed and these flowers give glorious colour to Tashkent's streets and squares in May and June.

As new plantings were set in place, so old plantings disappeared. Once, Tashkent was characterised by the thousands of fruit-trees, particularly apricots, which made an unforgettable scene in spring on the hillsides of the Ming-Uryuk district. Intense archaeological excavations during the 1950s brought a radical landscape change when most of the fruit-trees were uprooted.

It is hard to comprehend the landlocked isolation of Tashkent. To the south lies the sub-continent of India, to the east the distances of Tibet and China, to the north the wastes of Siberia, to the west Persia and to the north-west all Europe. Yet, in this place I had glimpses of the Garden of Eden.

Previously unpublished

Extract from Nina's travel diary

First impressions of Tashkent, 12 April, 1985:

The dramatic impression was of greenery – all the trees were in leaf or blossom and the Judas Tree was everywhere in its pink-purple splendour. Neat dark cypresses, cone-shaped, afforded a foil for the grass and young green of the oaks and mulberries.

Moorish gardens in Spain

The old gardens of Cordoba, Seville and Granada have modern variations in the colourful courtyards of Andalusia and in the patios of California. Moorish style gardens are favourites of mine.

They appeal to the senses and to the intellect. The discipline in their design commands respect, the economy of scale is impressive and symmetry came naturally to people interested in mathematics and building.

There is sensual delight in jets of water sparkling in sunlight and in the ripple and drip of that most precious resource of the Arab world. When the fountains are still and the moon rises, mysterious reflections float over the courtyard pools.

The Moors were influenced by the Persian 'paradise garden' and its symbolism – particularly the *char bagh* or four-section garden, created by intersecting water channels. This suggested the division of the universe described in Genesis '… and a river went out of Eden to water the garden and thence it was parted and became into four heads'. Walled for protection from dusty summer winds and bitter winter gales, the paradise garden offered seclusion for entertainment, dalliance and meditation.

I like to visit the Moorish gardens of Spain in the order of their development. First, Cordoba where orange trees were planted nine centuries ago in the court of ablutions by the entrance to the great mosque. The strong sunlight emphasises the glossy leaves and glowing fruit and the trees look agreeable beside the bulk of the building. This Patio de los Naranjos is one of the oldest walled gardens in Europe.

Unfortunately, other gardens near Cordoba – those of the

court city of Medina Azahara – are in ruins. Restoration is now being attempted and enthusiastic garden historians have a field day in this delightful spot.

In Seville, the flowers of Persia – oleanders, roses, irises and carnations – bring colour and fragrance to the garden of the Alcazar. Cypress trees, symbolising death, and almond trees, representing life, provide cool arcades for strolling. Tiled benches for resting give pleasure to all who enter.

Decorative tiles became a feature of Moorish gardens. They maintain colour when flowers wither in the increasing heat or are absent in winter. Just as the Persians sought to perpetuate the beauty of their gardens by weaving glorious carpets to be 'flowers for winter', so the Moors designed tiles.

Granada, once described as 'a goblet full of emeralds', has the best-known Moorish gardens. Set in the foothills of the Sierra Nevada, its strategic position favoured the building of fort, palace and garden.

The Alhambra contains strongly architectural gardens in pure Moorish style – the Courtyard of the Lions and the Courtyard of the Myrtles – with pool and surrounding arcades where superbly carved pillars and vaults suggest palm trees in an oasis. There are few flowers and the 'red fort' exudes a no-nonsense masculine aura.

The Generalife is part of the summer palace which is lighter, softer and more intimate than the Alhambra. The gardens as a whole have a dream-like quality, yet each has its own persona.

In the Courtyard of the Cypresses, the pool and fountain do not dominate the enclosed space in the traditional way. The garden itself is a pool of darkness where the ancient trees create a sense of mystery, intrigue and romance as befits a legendary trysting place.

A puckish humour and great engineering skills are apparent in the Camino de las Cascades. Water flows down conduits formed by the balustrade and open stone banisters of the stairway. It gurgles and rushes along with increasing speed and musical sound. Small basins, each with a tiny fountain, decorate the landings and establish the Moorish character of the structure.

The most famous garden of the Generalife is the Patio de la Acequia – the Courtyard of the Long Pool. Succeeding centuries have seen modification and alteration to the original, but in detail rather than design. The proportions of this elegant garden are perfectly attuned to the building containing it. A marble-lined pool, forty-nine metres long, is the central feature.

On my first visit, thirty years ago, clipped yews gave an Italianate feeling to the courtyard. Today graceful jets of water in the Moghul tradition give sound and movement. Banks of myrtle, roses and carnations reinforce the linear perspective, almost like an English herbaceous border. But the changing tastes or trends in planting are superficial; the *char bagh* characteristics remain at the heart of the garden.

By noon in summer the courtyard is oppressively hot and claustrophobic. This is the moment to go to the mirador. It gives a panoramic view of the *vega*, the great Andalusian plain, shimmering without horizon in the heat.

Set against seeming infinity of plain, or in arid desert, or amidst concrete metropolis, a Moorish garden is a precious and private place.

Previously unpublished

Royal Botanic Gardens, Hobart

Established: c. 1828; Area: 13.5 hectares; Highlights: native trees, convict-built wall, conservatory, Fuchsia House, Lily Pond.

Walls give presence and aesthetic appeal to any garden. Their solidity counterpoints the fragile, ephemeral quality of flowers; their sun-drenched stones contrast with the cool, shadowy pattern of leaves; their very familiarity is a foil for the mysterious distance of a receding vista.

Convict-built walls in the oldest Australian botanic gardens, Sydney and Hobart, suggest the early governors were interested in botany, keeping the felons usefully employed and protecting the precincts of Government House.

In 1829 Governor Arthur gave orders for building the interesting wall which today borders the approach to the main gates of The Royal Botanic Gardens, Hobart. It was designed to form a boundary to the Queen's Domain and to be an internally heated wall on which exotic fruits and flowers could be grown – a popular notion in nineteenth century English kitchen gardens.

The wall is double-sided. Visitors to the gardens see a surface of freestone blocks. On the other side, faced with brick, you can see the fire-place apertures and air-ducts which assisted the distribution of warmth from the coal fires burning in the fire-places.

Stone from the Old Hobart General Hospital was used to build the fine conservatory. Here changing floral displays mark the seasons. Winter is bright with Cyclamen, Cinerarias and *Primula malacoides*; spring brings Calceolarias, Schizanthus and

Primula obconica; summer shows Tuberous Begonias, Hydrangeas, Cymbidium orchids, Impatiens, Lobelia and Coleus while autumn boasts Chrysanthemums, Tuberous Begonias and Coleus.

A further delight of the Hobart gardens is the variety of native trees – *Phyllocladus asplenifolius* (the Celery Top Pine), *Dacrydium Franklinii* (the Huon Pine), *Athrotaxus selaginoides* (the King William Pine), the Diselma Pine and *Eucalyptus globulus*, the state's floral emblem. Two beautiful flowering trees, the Native Laurel and the Leatherwood, loved by bees and honey-fanciers, can be seen in the Fern House.

The gardens were handed over to the Royal Society of Tasmania in 1844. This encouraged members to take a personal interest in their development. The Tasmanian botanist, Ronald Campbell Gunn donated his herbarium and eighty-eight rare Asiatic plants were presented by Sir Joseph Hooker who had been plant-collecting in Tasmania.

Much more recently Rutgers University gave an American Dogwood (*Cornus florida* var. *rubra*) to commemorate a visit by the alumni in the US Bicentennial Year. Polish ex-servicemen living in Hobart presented a Polish Larch (*Larix polonica*).

The Fuchsia House built in 1958 resulted from donations of materials, labour and service on the part of many supporters of the gardens. It houses sixteen different varieties including *Fuchsia corymbiflora* 'Alba' and *F. triphylla*.

There are some 'curiosities' in the Hobart gardens and

The 'Arthur Wall'. Courtesy Royal Tasmanian Botanical Gardens.

although not to everyone's taste, they too show a popular interest. The stone archway was made for the AMP Society's original building in 1913. It was donated to mark the 150th Anniversary of the gardens. The floral clock built by cadets at the Science Centre of the Education Department was installed in 1968.

The unusual fountain, *Antipodean Voyage*, commemorates the bicentenary of the beginning of French exploration in Tasmanian waters. It is made from Huon Pine, which is remarkably durable in water. The fountain highlights the place of water in the design of the gardens.

An artificial stream with rapids and rocky edges creates a miniature landscape in which low-growing shrubs and creeping ground cover look well against more distant conifers or poplars.

The original storage dam has been re-landscaped several times. Now the Lily Pond, it is one of the most attractive areas in the gardens. Cordyline palms, Doryanthes, *Tetrapanax papyriferus* 'Variegata', and Cynara surround the pool. The dramatic *Gunnera manicata* and the slender *Arundo donax* 'Variegata' complement each other to perfection. Colour comes from the Nymphaea – white, gold and red – and from plantings of annuals such as marigolds, salvia and ageratum.

Small is beautiful and many Tasmanians have demonstrated a personal interest in their Botanic Gardens. Visitors will long remember plantings by wall and by water.

Previously unpublished

Darling Harbour's Friendship Garden

One of the few public Chinese gardens in the world which has been built outside the Chinese mainland, the Chinese Friendship Garden at Darling Harbour in Sydney, is a joint project of the sister cities of Guangzhou and Sydney. Designed in China, the garden was built by New South Wales craftsmen and was opened for the Bicentennial celebrations last year.

From outside, the Friendship Garden appears a conglomeration of buildings, walls and rocks dwarfed by city skyscrapers, hi-tech exhibition halls and overlooked by monorail and freeway. Within, a very different world awaits the visitor.

Buildings are an integral part of the Chinese garden and their construction and decoration are carefully chosen to frame selectively a view for quiet contemplation. But the garden is also for exploring and with its hills and rocks this can be physically demanding and quite exhilarating. Moreover the garden designer sees the passage through the garden as an allegorical journey calling for intellectual involvement.

The garden is full of symbolism – rocks represent mythical beasts, bridges and gateways mark the frontiers of new worlds. Thus some visitors may miss pleasurable dimensions of the garden. The guidebook which explains each of the six sections of the garden is a worthwhile investment for five dollars.

The Courtyard of Welcoming Fragrance is a delight – pebble paving in a traditional set flower pattern, three craggy rock sculptures set dramatically against a wall with intricately carved grilles which, by revealing something of the space beyond, entice one to continue inside.

Planted in the courtyard are the Lohan Tree (*Podocarpus macrophylla*), symbol of longevity and survival, the Fujian Flower Tree (*Osmanthus fragrans*) deliciously scented, Heavenly Bamboo (*Nandina domestica*), *Kerria japonica* and *Punica granatum.*

From the courtyard of the Hall of Longevity the prospective journey by the Lake of Brightness to the mountain pavilions is apparent. It stimulates the visitor to move on and meet the challenge but the neighbouring Lenient Jade Pavilion holds the visitor back with its attractive view over the Lotus Pool where the golden carp break the still surface of the water. Thus a dilemma is posed for the visitor to resolve.

A steep, rocky staircase leads up to the elegant Round Pavilion which gives an extensive view over the garden emphasising the tension between the serene views from the buildings and the physical challenge of the garden outside. Carved on the floor of the Round Pavilion is the yin and yang, symbol of this conflict.

My favourite part of the garden is The Chamber of Clear Rhythm, shaded by a loquat tree, and the Reading Brook Pavilion, surrounded by a cloud wall and bamboo grove. In the wall is a traditional moon-gate which frames a vista of the mountain pavilions and is itself framed by the shadowy tracery of bamboo stems. It is a garden within a garden, protected and peaceful, yet the swiftly flowing water cascading from the mountain-top lures one onward.

The Twin Pavilions (of Pear Fragrance and Litchie Shadow) exemplify the friendship and co-operation between the province of Guandong and the state of New South Wales. Growing around the pavilions are plants of Chinese origin, litchies and flowering cherries, and a single waratah symbolising New South Wales.

The jewel in the garden is the Clear View Pavilion set among a pine and cedar grove on the summit of the mountain above the waterfall. It is a double-storied building decorated with fine carvings of the 'three friends of winter' (the pine, the bamboo and the plum) as well as flowers of Guandong.

After passing through the Mountain Gate, guarded by a 'lion' rock and a 'horse' rock, the pilgrim enters the Stone Forest, a land of many legends and a strange foreboding. A traditional drum bridge marks the end of the forest and a return to the placid Lake of Brightness where the Peace Boat Pavilion appears to float.

The plants in the garden do not dominate the landscape. They are integrated with buildings, rocks, courtyards and water. Colour, shape, density, foliage texture, height, fragrance and symbolic meaning are the factors that govern the choice of a particular plant.

Evergreens are used for unifying different sections of the garden and the relationship between plants and water is carefully controlled – willows are tilted towards the water and the setting of water-lilies or lotuses never mars the clear reflections of pavilions. The fragility of plants is emphasised by placing them in precarious positions against rocks. At the foot of a waterfall there is a frangipani.

Where it is used, ground colour is strong. The Chinese consider red and gold as 'lucky' colours and ixoras and clivias provide the red while allamanda gives the gold.

The counterbalancing forces of yin and yang are everywhere in the garden – in the contrast of light and shadow, enclosed space and open space, in stone and water, and in mountains and valleys.

Like the Brisbane Japanese Garden which was transported from the 1988 Expo site to Mount Cootha, the Chinese Garden at Darling Harbour is a significant legacy from our Bicentennial year.

Previously unpublished

Close to home

Close to home: introduction

Nina Crone lived most of her life in Melbourne. Upon retirement from Melbourne Girls Grammar School, she moved to a property she owned in Walkerville, South Gippsland (Victoria), where she lived for ten years before returning once again to Melbourne in 2005.

This section of the book celebrates Nina's writings and reflections on flora and their connections with the lives of Melburnians and the citizens of Gippsland that were published in the pages of *The Age*. Descriptions are provided and stories told about gardens and open spaces in Melbourne and Gippsland, the botanical icons of the city of Melbourne, and plant and garden festivals that took place in both locations.

For the first few years that Nina lived in Gippsland, local gardens and botanical events became the focus of her interest. She also designed and constructed a magnificent garden on her Walkerville property and described the processes she experienced doing so in the pages of *The Age*. In 1997, the last articles she wrote for *The Age* appeared in print, after which she began targeting and publishing her writings about the history of various Australian plants and gardens in the journal, *Australian Garden History*. Nina was appointed the editor of that journal in 2001, a position she held until mid-2006.

Also included in this section is an eclectic cluster of articles that can loosely be categorised as having an 'educational' focus. In these contributions, Nina clearly communicates information and promotes resources, career options, and learning opportunities related to the botanical world. Whether consciously or not, her true vocation as an educator of extraordinary talent is apparent in all her writings.

Helen Forgasz

MELBOURNE

Following the tree trail

Celebrate the Year of the Tree by following an American tree trail in the Royal Botanic Gardens.

From Gate C, head towards the Eastern Lawn. Just before you reach the shelter there is a bed on your left which contains two *Liriodendron tulipifera* (Tulip Tree). The tree bears beautiful pale-green flowers in late spring or early summer. It is an excellent honey plant, as the average 20-year-old tree is estimated to produce 3.5 kilograms of nectar. It can reach a height of more than 50 metres, so it was useful as a source of timber for pioneers. In America, the tulip tree rarely grows west of the Mississippi River.

Continuing downhill along the path skirting the Eastern Lawn, notice on your left a graceful medium-sized tree, *Fraxinus americana* (White Ash). Cross the lawn at this point towards the bulb bed in the Central Lawn to find the slow-growing *Aesculus pavia* (Red Buckeye), which was planted by the pianist Ignace Paderewski during a visit to Melbourne in 1904. The buckeye family contains such species as *A. glabra* (Ohio Buckeye) and *A. californica* (Californian Buckeye) and is a common tree in the Ohio Valley.

Walk towards the lake, keeping the bulb bed on your left. In the large bed on your right there are two trees which provide splendid color in the autumn. *Acer saccharinum* (Silver Maple) grows profusely in the North Eastern States of America and is related to *Acer saccharum* (Sugar Maple), the source of maple syrup during 'sugarin' weather' when the sap responds to spring and rises in the maple trunks. The sugar maple is the official tree of New York State, West Virginia and Wisconsin. *Liquidambar styraciflua* (Sweet Gum) is a handsome deciduous tree.

Now follow the path left along the lake to the William Tell shelter, and then take the path to the left towards the fern gully. Notice the towering tree at the foot of the gully. This is *Taxodium mucronatum* (Montezuma Bald Cypress), a native of Mexico. Taxodiums are water-loving and often grow in water, developing buttresses around their trunk and curious conical projections called 'knees' which are raised above water-level from outlying roots to enable the trees to breathe.

Continue up the hill towards the Oak Lawn and turn left to reach the Magnolia Bed where a large *Carya illinoinensis* (Pecan Tree) is found. This tree grows widely in the southern states of America, and is the state tree of Texas. The distinctively flavored pecan nut features in many regional dishes. The tree was respected by the American Indians as a manifestation of the Great Spirit.

Planted in the same bed are several varieties of the dogwood family. *Cornus sericea* (American Dogwood) is clearly labelled, but also seek out *Cornus florida pendula*, a weeping variety of the flowering dogwood, on the bed on the southern side of the path. Flowering dogwood is a plant for all seasons. In spring white blossoms, in summer bright green leaves, in autumn a fiery red end and in winter a tracery of branches.

Turn back along the path towards the Oak Lawn, and notice a tall spruce in the bed backing on to the nursery and workshop area. This tree is *Picea sitchensis* (Sitka Spruce), the state tree of Alaska where it grows to a considerable size. Further along is a slender tree on the lawn to the left. In late September striking deep purplish-pink flowers cover the branches. *Cercis siliquastrum* (Judas Tree) gained its popular name from the legend that Judas Iscariot hanged himself from its branches.

Cross the Oak Lawn in the direction of the Australian Border to discover *Quercus macrocarpa* (Burr Oak), the state tree of Illinois where it dominates the rolling hills. Easily recognisable among the oaks is *Magnolia grandiflora* (Southern Magnolia) with its leathery short-pointed leaves shining deep green on the upper surface and a rusty velvet below. This tree, one of eight magnolias native to Eastern USA, is redolent of the Old South and was frequently cultivated in the garden of plantation homesteads. President Andrew Jackson planted a *Magnolia Grandiflora* near the portico of the White House in memory of his wife, Rachel.

Leaving the Oak Lawn, continue down the path towards the Hopetoun and Huntingfield lawns where examples of American pines are found. *Cupressus macrocarpa* (Spreading Monterey Pine) is a feature of the Hopetoun Lawn – indeed so well has this species adapted to Victoria that it is often more impressive than those pines growing on the Monterey Peninsula of California. Further along the lawn the towering trunks of *Pinus radiata* (Monterey Pine) and *Pinus ponderosa* (Western Yellow Pine) are clearly visible.

The latter is the state tree of Montana, although it grows in every state from the western edge of the Great Plains to the Pacific. On 4 July 1876, in a small Arizona settlement, lumberjacks stripped the branches from a tall ponderosa pine to run up the American flag with rawhide strings. The tall flagpole became such a well-known landmark that it gave the name to the town – Flagstaff.

There are many more American trees in the Royal Botanic Gardens and although winter finds some denuded of foliage it is well worth returning to see them in leaf or flower or fruit.

The Age, 8 October 1982, Weekender, p. 6.

The towering Montezuma Bald Cypress at the foot of Fern Gully in 2008, Royal Botanic Gardens, Melbourne. Photographer: Helen Forgasz.

Perennial border, Royal Botanic Gardens, Melbourne. Photographer: Nina Crone.

The two imposing *Eucalyptus citriodora* at the north end of Swanston Street, Melbourne, in 2007. Photographer: John Botham.

The Kitchen Garden, Venus Bay. Photographer: Nina Crone.

Morwell Rose Garden: 'Tequila Sunrise' spilling out over a traffic roundabout in 2007. Photographer: Helen Botham

Algerian oak (left) and London plane (right) stand guard over the 'sound shell' at Mossvale Park, Gippsland, in 2008. Photographer: Helen Botham.

Before Nina planted her Walkerville garden, December 1990. Photographer: Nina Crone.

Nina's Walkerville garden is well established, 2005. Photographer: Nina Crone

A question of identity

Rainbow hues are brightening the Royal Botanic Gardens as the bedding areas display their treasures: pink and white primulas, gold and velvety brown pansies near the Nareeb Gates and in that most sheltered part of the gardens – between the lilly-pilly hedge and the glasshouses – stocks and cinerarias.

The subtle gradations of purple, puce, blue, crimson, mauve and pale pink enhance the textural counterpointing of upright stocks and the upturned florets of the cinerarias with their glowing color.

At the junction of two paths is a triangle of pastel-soft polyanthus – cream, primrose, salmon, rose-pink, mauve and bronze – and in the distance the last of the daffodils sway cheerfully on the Oak Lawn. The colors in my paintbox were never as bright as these.

The Age, 25 November 1986, p. 29.

Nature flourishes amid the city's heavy traffic

In surprising ways workaday Melbourne refreshes the senses. Nature flourishes among our network of asphalt and concrete, or is displayed in utilitarian buildings, and our climate bestows a pattern of change through the year.

Traffic snarls and red lights can lead to pleasurable discoveries. I never regret heavy traffic or a mandatory stop at the Punt Road–Alexandra Avenue intersection. The elm on the south-west corner is magnificent in any season. The branches have been thinned, braced and shaped to perfection. The canopy, ready to scatter the seeds, appears to bear green blossom. You need to be waiting for the Clifton Hill bus to appreciate the path under the elm. It is edged by a mixed border of bluebells, forget-me-nots, cinerarias, clivias, bearded irises and arum lilies.

On the other side of the city, traffic traces out the roundabout where the north end of Swanston Street swings into College Crescent. Easing into the slow lane you can admire two imposing *Eucalyptus citriodora* on the traffic island. Smooth, silver-grey trunks stretch towards a bleached Australian sky. Imagination moves away from urban pollution to dusty inland plains. The other delight of this species, the lemon scent of the leaves, escapes you in a car.

Plant fragrance is ephemeral and too often lost to the city dweller. Seeking strongly perfumed species to compete with chemical emissions, we plant lilac in a corner of the garden, jasmine on the fence, lily-of-the-valley as groundcover and boronia by the patio.

But grow one species by the thousand and you have a different experience. The pervasive, understated fragrance which rises from the slopes of Tesselaar's flower farm at Silvan early in October is unforgettable. It comes from row upon row of misty-hued hyacinths.

Gather enough cut flowers of one family, keep them in a cool, closed place and you will find a perfume you have never noticed. The annual Iris Society show in November is remarkable for the subtle scent emanating from the rainbow-colored blooms displayed in a functional concrete hall.

For visual pleasure, there is nothing better than the Spring Festival held around Show Week at David Jones in Bourke Street, where thousands of flowers make a spectacular picture. Perfect specimens of old favorites – roses, gladioli, carnations, daisies, forget-me-nots and primulas – interspersed with peonies, tulips and magnolias, contrast with exotic orchids, strelitzia and torch ginger. Individually, each pot, vase or hanging basket is artistry in texture, color, line or form. This year my favorite arrangement combined the feathery green and gold flowers of leucodendron with glossy monstera leaves, gold-flecked foliage of *Aucuba japonica*, trails of ivory and sprigs of wintersweet.

Strangely, it is rain, that most maligned characteristic of Melbourne, which enhances the sight and scent of nature in our city. Rain heightens the fragrance of wattle in August, it saturates the fallen leaves in April making a pungent autumn smell, it glistens on bare branches in June, it washes dust off the hydrangeas in December and it drives us indoors to appreciate our cut flowers.

The Age, 15 October 1985, Melbourne Living, p. 6.

Exploring our squares is rewarding

The drinking fountain in Victoria Square is elaborate. 'For God, Home and Country', it was presented to the Melbourne City Council by the Women's Christian Temperance Union of Victoria in 1901. Now the Melbourne City Council has given Victoria Square to the state as the latest area set aside for pedestrian enjoyment.

The young plane trees will give shade in summer and allow for sun in winter. They continue the treescape that has moved from Collins Street to the precincts of the State Offices to the Civic Square and to Elizabeth and Lonsdale streets, adding elegance to the city as well as marking the changing seasons.

It is a rewarding experience to explore Melbourne's squares. (Lest anyone contest the definition, I used a street directory to determine them.) They are within healthy walking distance of each other in the city or Carlton area.

Most squares in Melbourne have evolved from an area of grass, trees and diagonal paths established in the late 19th century. By 1900 it was fashionable to add a commemorative drinking fountain, the 1930s brought lawn bowling clubs, with the 1950s came children's playgrounds and the 1970s introduced festas and 'happenings', and FEIPP [Free Entertainment in Public Places].

Notices in Curtain Square advise that 'dogs must be leashed', and the area is surrounded by a cyclone fence to keep the dogs out and the children in. On the playcentre a stone, laid in 1957, reminds us that community action and civic responsibility contributed to the development and use of this open space. However, except for an imposing avenue of 12 Moreton Bay figs (*Ficus macrophylla*), little remains of the original planting.

The drinking fountain in Victoria Square, Melbourne, in 2007. Photographer: John Botham.

Macarthur Square is like an out-sized median strip enhanced by 10 pairs of magnificent elm trees. It is a fine place for dreaming on the grass or reading in the sun.

The traditional form of Murchison Square is complemented by the surrounding houses, the blue-stone lanes and the careful domestic planting, which softens the angular building. Kerbside prunus trees effectively counterpoint the greenery, giving a sense of variety and harmony.

Today the Victoria Bowling Club occupies the northern end of University Square so that imagination is needed to picture the original green forecourt that once graced the main entrance to Melbourne University in Grattan Street. From the southern end of the square, an avenue of elms leads to the drinking fountain built 'in recognition of faithful service rendered by Thomas Ferguson, secretary of the Melbourne Total Abstinence Society from 1868–1904'. The path continues towards tables with chequered tops for chess and draughts.

To the east, Pelham Street leads to Lincoln Square, an updated area. On the Swanston Street side a fountain sparkles in the centre of the paved plaza, backed by geraniums, lantana, correa, kangaroo paw, berberis and photinia. Lawns slope towards Bouverie Street where roses – 'Superstar', 'Masquerade' and 'Marlena' – make a bright display in the rose gardens.

Further east still, Pelham Street reaches Argyle Square. Here, ground has been lost to the Carlton Bowling Club which, on the Lygon Street side, is hidden behind a cheerful border of polyanthus, snapdragons, ranunculus and roses. The vestige of the original square – grass, elms, diagonal paths, and memorial drinking fountain to a long-standing resident – comes into its own as a fairground each November during the Lygon Street Festa.

Melbourne's most recent squares, Civic and Victoria, owe more to the Mediterranean tradition of fountains, paving stones and container plants, than to the English tradition of grass and elms. Squares are more than green places. The best have an architectural integrity that offsets the open space and most are now used for community activities. Many reflect our migrant origins with a nostalgia for a village green or an Italian piazza.

At the corner of Victoria and Elizabeth streets, Victoria Square is not a verdant place, but it is full of atmosphere. The renovated meat hall of the nearby market, the lamp-posts, the iron stanchions, the restored shop veranda canopies and the old drinking fountain contribute significantly.

Doubtless the Christian Temperance women and the secretary of the Total Abstinence Society would frown on the conviviality of Lygon Street and the frivolity in Victoria Square, but Breughel would delight in the use Melbourne is now making of its open spaces, whether shaded by elm or plane tree.

The Age, 7 January 1986, p. 16.

Delight and inspiration at Garden Week 1986

Spectacular arrangements of fruit, vegetables and flowers provided an appropriate portal to Garden Week 1986. The prodigality and creative endeavor of that display was sustained in other areas of the show.

For the second successive year, Garden Week was held at the College of Agriculture and Horticulture, Burnley. It was wise to use the same venue again and a different style emerged.

This year's displays fitted more comfortably into the permanent garden environment. Thoughtful planning integrated the exhibition as a whole, in contrast to 1985, when commercial areas were isolated from garden areas.

There was no doubt that the show had grown. The State Government and *The Sun* newspaper added their support to the efforts of the Nurserymen's Association of Victoria, of the Victorian College of Agriculture and Horticulture (VCAH) and of the individual exhibitors.

More discrimination in the presentation of displays complemented a better use of space. The subtle greens and varied textures of rockery plants, conifers, herbs and indoor plants counterpointed the color of dahlias, carnations and gladioli in one marquee, of tulips, freesias and hyacinths in another and of roses, orchids and proteas in a third place.

The special displays – the Cottage Garden, the Herb Garden, the Sunken Garden, the Rose Garden and the Water Garden – brought fresh delight and inspiration.

As well as the pleasure of living plants, Garden Week offered useful information on hydroponic gardening, tissue culture propagation, turf and tools. Special interest groups set up displays of plants appropriate to concerns of ecologists.

The pamphlet 'Melbourne's Original Gardens' linked native species with geological areas such as the basalt plains, the sand belt or the coastal fringe. This commendable initiative was associated with displays of the listed plants.

Because publicity for Garden Week described it as 'an invaluable exhibition for garden lovers and enthusiasts of all ages', I took sixth-grader Rebecca and her younger sister Rachel to Burnley. They gave gold stars to the rose garden, the cactus and the bonsai displays. It was evident, too, that the 'Black Magic' pansy, the 'Red Devil' leucadendron and the topiary elephant captured their imagination. At one of the book stalls Rebecca was interested in *The Complete Carrot* while Rachel favored *Earthworms*.

The final day of Garden Week was the first day of Senior Citizens' Week and special activities were arranged at Burnley for that age group. Perhaps a future Garden Week might include a children's day to provide more activities for young gardeners. Seed-collecting expeditions, seed-planting and propagating activities and an exhibition trail are possibilities.

Generally, support services at the show were good – easy parking, a creche, canteen and bistro facilities – but I am sure visitors would welcome forward publication of the subject matter for lectures and demonstrations, as well as a clearer map showing the location of exhibits.

Garden Week 1986 was a bigger, brighter and more diverse undertaking than previously. Professional help

Illustrator: Glenda Romeril.

was engaged to stage it. Such assistance is only as good as the brief given. The aim of the week must be considered and its relationship to other exhibitions.

If Burnley continues to be the chosen venue, organisers need to decide whether to segregate activities as in 1985, or integrate them as in 1986. The former emphasises the natural beauty of the Burnley Gardens, the latter provides a greater 'showground' atmosphere.

ALISON DALRYMPLE teaches at a Melbourne girls' secondary school. She is interested in gardening as a form of creative endeavor and, in terms of history, as the representation of an age.

The Age, 18 March 1986, p. 27.

Measuring success by the departing plants

G arden Week 1987 settled into its Burnley site for the third year with greater assurance and confidence. There was a more comfortable relationship between the historic gardens and the commercial displays.

New this year was a keynote theme; the choice of Japan as a feature was a good one.

The keynote theme, carefully handled, is a sound idea for it ensures that each Garden Week is not just more of what was offered previously. It will be interesting to see whether it is continued in the future. Plants and gardens must remain the *raison d'être* of Garden Week and for that reason I was thankful that the advertised dancers and cookery demonstrators did not seem to materialise.

Credit must go to those exhibitors who spared a thought for children – Dr T's Lawn Clinic with its dolls' picnic on the grass, the hairy, bespectacled characters among the succulents, the budgies by the gazebo and Henderson's 'Kid's Corner' seed packets.

Visitors to Garden Week expect an impressive contribution from the Victorian College of Agriculture and Horticulture. (Remember the international vegetable gardens of 1985 and the specialist gardens of 1986?) They were not disappointed. The 'Backyard Landscaping Displays' attracted many favorable comments and provided practical ideas for planting schemes, reminding us of the fine educational work being done on the Burnley campus.

Another significant contribution to Garden Week is that of the conservation groups. Displays showed the work being done in the western suburbs, in the Yarra Bank revegetation project, the Merri Creek project, the City of Sandringham and the Victorian Indigenous Nurseries Cooperative.

The sponsor of the Garden Week booklet this year, the Board of Works, warned us that Victoria will only remain the Garden State through better management of its water resources. Many stands in the exhibition reiterated this message in practical terms by demonstrating mulches, timers, drip systems and micro-sprays.

Visitors appreciated the increased pedestrian space, the clearer signposts and the listing of lectures and demonstrations in the program. Given, too, the vagaries of Melbourne's weather in March, the VCAH Hall is a better venue

Illustrator: Glenda Romeril.

for demonstrations than last year's open tent.

The ultimate success of Garden Week lies with those who surge out of Burnley hugging huge stag's head ferns, dwarfed by showy Mandevillas, clutching spiral stakes like spears, and juggling bright showbags of bulbs or bulky micro-watering kits.

It lies, too, in the interest given to those who bring their lack-lustre and ailing leaves to the expert for advice – and it lies in educating our children to love and care for plants.

A lively response to living things was the essence of Garden Week 1987. That response will be reflected for many years in gardens throughout Melbourne.

The Age, 17 March 1987, p. 23.

Themes full of visual delight

Garden Week Expo 1988 developed further a strength of previous Garden Weeks – the theme garden. In the hands of professional marketing management, this idea made for unified, direct presentation full of visual delight.

Just as knowing visitors to the Chelsea Flower Show immediately head for the marquee, so I believe visitors to the Burnley Show headed for the design gardens.

The garden design theme was evident the moment you saw Jenny Walker's formal French bedding display with white begonias, red celosia in parterre design around an elegant fountain.

Inner city dwellers found inspiration in the city courtyard garden, or the rooftop container garden, the art garden or the oriental influence garden. Projects combined the talents of a nursery, a landscape contractor and various suppliers, making for a far more effective display than separate 'trade stands'. Visitors could easily refer to their passport-style program for details.

The proximity of the display gardens allowed excellent comparison in the use of materials, like decking, paving or fencing. The overall impression was one of stylishness, professionalism and sophistication.

A 'Gardener's Quality Market' offered a comfortable means of selecting living souvenirs at retail prices, while the allied trade exhibition marquee provided for other gardening needs.

There were gentle reminders of our Bicentenary year in the dominant position given to the Victorian era garden with its formal bedding pattern, precise edgings and cast iron accessories – fences, fountains, garden furniture and even a bridge. Other reminders of the Bicentenary were the birthday candle banksia display and the new cultivars among the kangaroo paws and the azaleas.

At every Garden Week there are corners that appeal to children. This year they enjoyed the turf maze, the Blinky Bill's Friends in the Bush Garden, the cactus display and Kevin Heinze's children's garden.

The displays set up for Garden Week did not intrude on the unique character of the Burnley site itself. Thanks to the autumn showers, never was the fragrance of the gardens so pervasive. The rose garden was heady with perfume which gave way to the more intriguing scents of the bush garden and then to the spicy smell of curry and herbal fragrances.

The harmony between the permanent plantings in the Burnley Gardens and the transitory displays of the Expo was well-judged. Each complemented and enhanced the other. The Nurseryman's Association of Victoria should have no doubt that the services of a development and management team is worthwhile.

More than 73,000 people attended the nine days of Garden Week, despite inclement weather and a transport strike. This is an increase of 13,000 on the previous year.

The Age, 22 March 1988, p. 26.

Garden Week has grand designs

Garden Week Expo now has the cachet of high fashion. This year it took 'design' as its theme and there was a designer label-quality about the presentation – assured and elegant.

The sign writing was stylish and it was a wise decision to keep the logo devised last year. Using the same motif for several years shows good business and marketing sense.

The site-plan and exhibitors' information sheet were easy to handle. I liked the brief notes on the non-commercial displays – the hosta border, the stream garden, the foliage border and the Victorian heritage woodland, to mention only a few.

This year the garden design area comprised displays, including four constructed with the help of Bicentennial grants. The Grass Garden attracted much attention and will undoubtedly be a trendsetter; the Victorian Garden highlighted the detailed research that is essential to achieve authenticity in a period garden; and a tongue-in-cheek humor was apparent in the Native Garden.

Asian influence was seen in the bonsai display, set out in the open against a white background exactly as in the nurseries of Nanjing or Hangzhou. The orchid display centred on the dainty Malay and Thai varieties.

Bands and other music groups added to the enjoyment of families picnicking on the lawns and the choice offered by the range of food outlets ensured that all tastes and time exigencies were met.

The bottom line of any expo is the *cost* of staging it in relation to the *return* – especially when, like Burnley, it is subject to the vagaries of weather and is of necessarily short duration. Moreover, Australia has a small population and suffers from the tyranny of distance, so Expo organisers must always seek new initiatives.

This year I enjoyed the Garden Week Expo as much as the Chelsea Flower Show, but in a different way. Certainly the breathtaking scale of exhibits in the grand marquee at Chelsea is unparalleled throughout the world, but the setting at Burnley compares more than favorably with the Ranelagh gardens. Chelsea is a spring show and Burnley an autumn one: each is memorable in its own way.

The Nurserymen's Association of Victoria and the Victorian College of Agriculture and Horticulture (Burnley) have done sterling work in bringing the Garden Expo to a commendably high standard. To reach further heights a wider perspective must be adopted.

I have seen the City of Singapore, the Channel Islands, Bermuda, and Philadelphia represented in the Chelsea Show as well as individual towns from the United Kingdom. There must be scope for national or international participation in Garden Expo. In an autumn show perhaps more could be made of fruit and vegetables (from Queensland, Tasmania, Hawaii, Japan).

Only through a national or regional orientation will the Burnley Expo rate a mention in the 'Kew Diary' that currently lists for 12 March this year – the time when our Garden Expo opened – the closing of the Philadelphia Flower Show (after eight days) and the closing of the Boston Flower Show (after nine days).

The Age, 21 March 1989, p. 25.

GIPPSLAND

Venus by the sea

ALISON DALRYMPLE visits an elegant garden by the sea.

The Kitchen Garden at Venus Bay in Gippsland is a splendid example of a coastal garden. Situated on the sand spit of Point Smythe at the mouth of the Tarwin River, it will inspire all who persevere with seaside gardens.

The sandy drive twists through thick tea-tree, passing an occasional gnarled *Banksia integrifolia*. Sound is muted. There is no view. A curious grey-green world engulfs you. It hones the senses, clears the mind, stimulates anticipation, excites curiosity.

This indigenous wilderness highlights the intimate, intensely private world of the cultivated garden. It counterpoints the organisation of exotic plantings.

The proportions of the Kitchen Garden are elegant and the scale is perfect. It may remind Melburnians of a *Botanica* display; Europeans may think of the Linnaeus House in Uppsala and Americans recall the vegetable garden at Mount Vernon.

Paula Green, who made the garden, declares she was not consciously influenced by any particular style. She was interested in a productive garden and 10 years ago planted the fruit trees and the original vegetables.

As they thrived and the garden expanded she realised she had discovered the secret of successful planting in a sandy, coastal area subject to Bass Strait gales. Paula believes this will be of most interest to visitors when the garden is open for Australia's Open Garden Scheme on 4–5 November. That is certainly so, but those with limited space for a garden and those with a flat site will find some worthwhile ideas, too.

This is a romantic garden full of memorable color harmonies and sheltered corners. It represents five years of intensive work on the owners' part.

Paula emphasises it is a high-maintenance garden where the sandy soil is constantly replenished with organic matter and where plants need nightly protection from kangaroos, wallabies and rabbits.

On the flat site with native bush denying any 'borrowed landscape', the use of architecture, garden structures, seats, tubs and pots is most effective.

Perimeter protection is imperative and this is imaginatively handled whether as hedging or fencing. *Lonicera nitida* graces the top of terraces of some gardens, rosemary and lavender species edge others. Inside the boundary fence Paula has planted a hazelnut hedge.

The Kitchen Garden shows how thoughtful planting can emphasise the beauty of vegetable foliage – the dark spikes of onion leaves contrasting with the leafy grey bulk of broad beans and the heavy purple heads of globe artichokes.

Companion borders of marigolds and pockets of Californian poppies (*Eschscholzia californica*) enliven this section of the garden.

In spring, the climber *Wisteria floribunda* 'Alba' binds the house to the garden, picking up the pure white of the tulips at the far end of the flower garden. Purple iris introduce a stronger color, while lilac continues the theme. Rich blue spikes of echium take over as leaves thicken on the wistaria. Plants with grey foliage, chosen to harmonise with the surrounding environment and because they will tolerate poor soils and dry conditions, edge many beds and provide contrast to the blaze of hot pink *Papaver somniferum* in late spring.

Gravel and flagstones solve the problem of traffic areas in sandy soil. Paula tells how stone, used also for retaining walls, drystone walls and edging, was individually selected at Ruby, 45 kilometres distant, and brought back 'in the ute'.

This is an organic garden using plants appropriate to the climate and the dry poor soil rather than 'specimens'. Where possible, recycled building materials are used, their weathered, comfortable quality contributing to the harmony of the whole.

Visitors can walk beyond the pickets of the Kitchen Garden to find the lily pond and continue on to the mangroves for a peaceful view of Anderson's Inlet.

For Paula Green this opening is her first venture into Australia's Open Garden Scheme. A perfectionist, she is excited about participating and explains: 'I have gained so much from visiting other people's gardens, I would like to offer something back.'

She believes the scheme is very important to gardeners. She says: 'A garden is a fragile vision and maintaining this vision over an extended period requires not only endurance but stimulation. Gardeners often work alone, and the scheme allows them to meet and interact with fellow gardeners to share knowledge.

'Balancing the variables of working with nature can be a difficult business, but it is the unpredictability of nature that keeps us humbled and hooked.'

Her garden makes an indelible impression on all who see it. For children it is 'The Secret Garden' come to life. All visitors will want to take home from this magic place one of the plants available for sale.

For attendant visitors not horticulturally inclined there is plenty to do in the area – surfing at Venus Bay, fishing or golfing by the Tarwin, bushwalking in the adjoining Point Smythe Reserve or sailing on Anderson's Inlet. But if ever a garden is to convert the philistines and convince the sceptics, it is this one.

The Age, 28 October 1995, Extra, p. 12.

Morwell's communal celebration in roses

P ut 2000 roses in the care of 30 volunteers on one hectare of
parkland that was once the cutting for the Morwell–Mirboo
North branch railway line, and you have a rose garden with a
difference.

The Morwell Centenary Rose Garden is not formal and
enclosed, but a very public place. It spills out joyously over
median strips and a traffic roundabout in Commercial Road,
covering them with 'Ralph's Creeper', 'Tequila Sunrise' or 'Rosy
Carpet'.

This rose garden, initiated in 1991, is not a council project
nor does it have government funding. It is a splendid example of
community commitment.

That so many people are involved engenders a sense of
personal ownership, responsibility and pride. Its location near
the central shopping district, as well as its proximity to a senior
citizen's centre, retirement village and nursing home, mean
visitors come both to experience and to learn from the roses.

Members of the management committee have expertise in
construction services, landscaping, horticulture, project
management, works supervision, secretarial work and in
marshalling community support. Trellis, pergolas and a new
arbor, for instance, were designed locally and made of donated
tubular material by apprentices sponsored by a local industry. At
this time of year, they are almost hidden by 'Talisman', 'Buff
Beauty' and 'Zepherine Drouhin'.

Requests to local groups for donations 'in kind' are
enthusiastically received, whether these be poultry manure,

construction materials or publicity and promotion. The Rose Society of Victoria has played an important and encouraging role throughout.

The plants are looked after by the Friends of Morwell Rose Garden. Each member receives a garden apron and is asked to care for more than 60 rose bushes. Time offered is the membership qualification. Duties are 'to inspect each rose bush weekly during the season and remove all spent blooms, to stake and tie new water shoots, to trim back any damaged or dead foliage and to observe if any bush is distressed due to lack of water, pests or disease or if a bush has been stolen'.

Watering, spraying, pruning, fertilising, weeding, edge-trimming and mowing are the responsibility of a maintenance panel led by Bob Jordan – a garden supervisor and apprentice help (one full-time or two part-timers). A regular newsletter is published as well.

Like Antoine de St Exupéry's 'little prince', all involved with the Morwell Rose Garden know that: 'It is the time you have wasted for your rose that makes your rose so important.' But they want to share their roses and they take great enjoyment in doing so.

The Age, 25 November 1995, Extra, p. 12.

The Strzelecki serenades

Summer, music and gardens go together, whether it is *Music for the People* in Melbourne, *Symphony under the Stars* in Sydney – or this weekend's *Music at Mossvale* in Gippsland's Strzelecki Ranges.

I find Mossvale Park welcoming in winter as well as summer, and beautiful in every season. It is a place of trees, carefully chosen trees that satisfy the senses. *Quercus, Catalpa, Liriodendron, Fagus, Betula, Tilia, Aesculus, Robinia, Fraxinus, Cryptomeria* are unexpected among the magnificent indigenous stands of peppermint gums, messmates, manna and mountain ash.

Immediately these trees tickle the visitor's curiosity. How did they and cedars, poplars, elms, lilacs, maples, chestnuts, ginkgo come to this unexpected spot near Mirboo North?

They came with a nurseryman named Francis Moss, who started two nurseries in Gippsland towards the end of last century after 35 years of running Mossmount Nursery at Buninyong, near Ballarat. The Mossvale Nursery was managed by one William Gould, who planted out the area that is now the public park. (And, incidentally, he trained the now feral ivy up tree trunks.)

Mossvale plant stock was renowned for its quality. The trees rejected for sale were used in the park area. During the 1920s, dairy cattle grazed among the Mossvale trees and, by the '30s, the area was increasingly used for picnics and sports. In 1946, it became a public reserve and is now managed by a local committee.

In 1969, the Grand March from *Tannhäuser* opened the first *Music in Mossvale Park*. The concert became an annual event, attracting more than 2000 people. In 1982, a sound shell was built, which musicians praise for its acoustic perfection.

The Moss family continues with another Mossmount nursery at Monbulk. Happily, it maintains a link with Mossvale through generous donations of young trees.

In 1987, four generations of the family were present to unveil a plaque honoring their indomitable forebear (and to plant four more trees).

Further plantings continue Mossvale's reputation as an arboretum. Its fine London plane tree (*Platanus* x *hispanica*), Oriental plane (*P. orientalis*), Algerian oak (*Quercus canariensis*) and chestnut-leaved oak (*Q. castaneifolia*) are listed on Victoria's register of significant trees.

Musicians serenade Mossvale's summer beauty, the pony club goes through its paces amid its splendid autumn display, winter travellers enjoy cheery fires in the sturdy stone shelter and, in spring, lovers marvel at the tender grass under the flowering cherries.

As for the pesky ivy by the river, may it be controlled rather than removed so that hobbits can move freely in Middle Earth and Tolkien fans offer a toast to the magic of Mossvale. My toast is to the memory of Francis Moss.

The Age, 24 February 1996, Extra, p. 12.

Making plans

*ALISON DALRYMPLE lays down the ground rules
for the gardener who wishes to employ a garden designer.*

Joining forces with a professional garden designer is a
rewarding experience and has many advantages.

Tasks are more speedily and efficiently accomplished;
professional experience avoids pitfalls that beset the amateur;
physically taxing tasks are carried out by machinery, specialist
sub-contractors and (for some of us) younger muscles. Most
importantly, someone else has an interest in the garden and a
vision of its future.

Good garden design does not come cheaply so it is
important to research the matter as thoroughly as you would a
new house, a new car, or a school for your child. Choose your
designer carefully. Look for rapport, someone *simpatico*.

Ideally you will know clearly what you want so you can
give a good brief and be realistic about costs, time and
preparation. But if you do not have any particular ideas, that's
fine, too. Your designer will prepare his or her own brief and
give good value but be careful that it is not in a trendy, short-
lived style. Garden writer Louisa Jones tells how designers fly
into the south of France to 'do' gardens for special events. That's
fine if you are a member of the glitterati, but not many of us are!

So, down to earth. I considered three designers. I asked to
see their work, checked their professional qualifications, had a
look at their own gardens and spoke to some of their clients.
Another consideration was specialist knowledge of local
conditions – soil type, climate, tradespeople, nurseries and other
suppliers.

What did my paragon of designers have to deal with? A flat

quarter hectare of patchy soil – heavy clay and poor sand – in a very windy area about a kilometre from the sea. Rainfall was reliable and abundant, indeed water tended to lie in parts of the site.

What did I want of the designer? To develop a concept plan for a garden characterised by plants suited to the Mediterranean climate (such as lavender, santolina, rosemary, sedums, westringias, liliums, echiums, roses, hebes, viburnums, and the ubiquitous agapanthus) with a patchy perimeter planting of native species. Vegetable, herb and fruit production should be provided for, and, once established, the garden should be low maintenance.

Elements were to include:

- a boundary planting of Australian species to suit the environment and provide a windbreak
- a front garden providing an outlook from the living room using the borrowed landscape of Waratah Bay and Wilson's Promontory
- retention of the vegetable garden
- the main decorative garden to the north with provision for herbs, roses and a border for the path to the front door.

Other considerations were the general drainage on the site, stabilisation and planting of the roadside embankment, and a support for climbers over the water tank.

In a preliminary discussion, I expressed likes and reservations – the idea of an informal herb garden was attractive, for instance, but I was afraid it would look dreary in winter when it was cut back. The concept plan was developed in October, allowing for extensive site work over summer and preparation for planting with the autumn rains.

Feeling it a demanding brief, I was anxious to see what the designer would produce. He delivered the plan on a Friday and there were some brilliant ideas. He put the herb garden on the north side of a wall so that its uninteresting winter hibernation was hidden from overlooking windows. The flatness of the site was countered by a stone wall, a raised 'show' bed, and by cleverly creating the Australian garden at a higher level. A bog garden soaked up the excess winter rains.

I had initial doubts about some aspects, and others I simply didn't like. So I followed my normal principle of three days consideration before a final decision. Over the weekend, my reservation about the width of the path in the north garden disappeared as I saw its possibilities. It conjured up games of petanque, and offered scope for pots overflowing with seasonal flowers or decorative citrus varieties. Now, I really would have to join the queue for Anduze jars.

But three days did not convert me to the idea of a sundial parterre in the east – this seemed monastic rather than Mediterranean. And I was not comfortable with the arrangement of the patio area. Those two areas, and the framework encasing the water-tank, were put on hold.

With the provisos accepted and the cheque written for this work, we proceeded to materials and costing. A significant factor was the stone to be used. Local stone was rejected as not

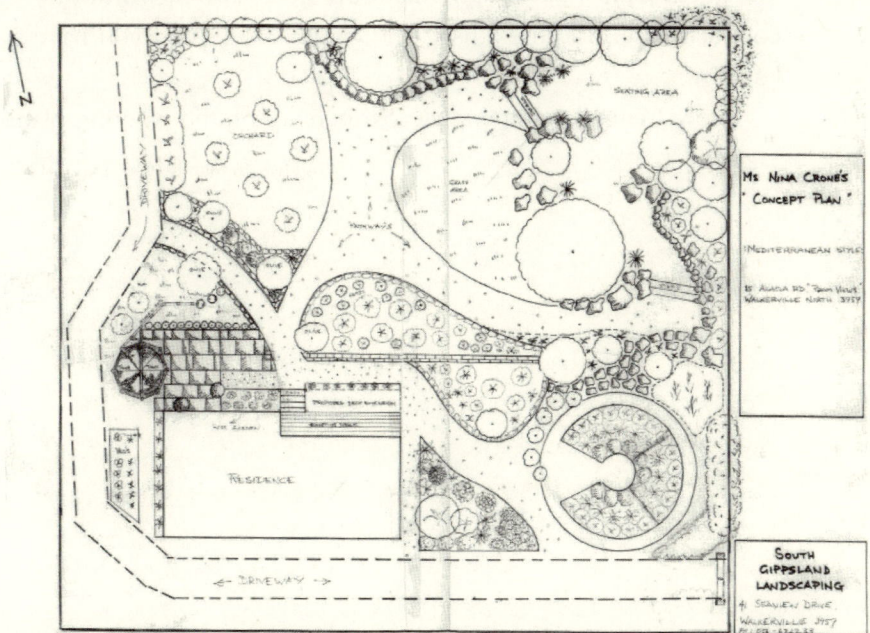

Landscape designer's plan for Nina's garden in Walkerville, 1995.

weathering well enough for walls, although acceptable as embedded boulders. Bluestone was too grim in color. Granite, from the Mornington Peninsula, seemed perfect with its warm golden tones. It was also the costliest item in the budget. Just as well I dropped the parterre and the patio!

Fine-tuning the cost estimate involved precise agreement on which plant stock was to be included, that any topsoil required would be additional, that installation of my gates from the old Flemington abattoirs and provision of mowing strips were included. The contract was signed and work began just before Christmas.

I kept a diary of progress and found my reactions swung from delight to doubt and back. It was most useful to do things in the garden while work was in progress, to appreciate the developing vistas and to help crystallise ideas for plantings. It also raised some practical problems, like getting the mower over rocky edgings, which could readily be solved at an early stage.

Working with a professional is exciting and stimulating. The ability of the trained designer to visualise the growth of the individual plants, particularly maturing trees, is well worth the contract price. Add the artistic and creative skills and you have a bargain.

Now I eagerly contemplate partnership on the planting plan.

The Age, 16 March 1996, Extra, p. 12.

Garden success stories

Nina Crone – retired school principal

My garden depends on tank water, so basic surface covers are a key to saving water for fruit trees and vegetables. I have three surfaces – grass, compacted gravel, leaves.

The grass is minimal – under the fruit trees and over the relm drain. The compacted gravel is maximal, indeed the drive and unusually broad garden paths seem disproportionate for a half-acre block. In South Gippsland, they weather the dry summers and soaking winters superbly, but leaf litter and koala droppings spoil their splendor.

So where most gardeners spend time mowing, I spend it raking. I cannot recommend a more pleasing activity. It affords wonderful thinking time (no noisy machines), gentle rhythmic exercise equalling tai chi, and it brings a rich horticultural reward.

Bark, leaves, needles, general detritus and twigs from Australian trees ranging from *Angophora costata* to *Casuarina stricta*, as well as koala and possum poo – all this is my third surface cover in the perimeter garden with its barbecue area.

The dry mixture, well trodden down, is aromatic and distinctly Australian. A topping of twigs and small branches minimises disturbance from wind. The same treatment makes the paths in the vegie patch delightfully soft underfoot.

After Operation Clean-up, Cover-up and Conserve Water, I can put down my rake and add plenty of ice to the drinks with a clear conscience.

The Age, 5 April 1997, Extra, p. 12.

Koala – at home in Nina's garden at Walkerville. Photographer: Nina Crone.

EDUCATIONAL MISCELLANY

Careers in horticulture

In the first of two articles, ALISON DALRYMPLE
gives advice on careers in horticulture and related disciplines.

So you are interested in the environment and looking for a career. Here are some suggestions.

1   Find the range of jobs or careers associated with the area of your interest. The CES (Commonwealth Employment Service) *Job Guide for Victoria 1984* published by the Australian Government Printing Service is invaluable – particularly Chapter 6, 'Job Titles Arranged in Interest Categories', and Chapter 7, 'Job Descriptions'.

2   List 15 or so possibilities. The following examples might help: Agricultural scientist, agricultural secretary, botanist, environmentalist, florist, flower grower, forester, fruitgrower, gardener, green keeper, horticultural advisor, horticulturist, landscape architect, landscape gardener, tree surgeon, turf manager, viticulturist.

3   Obtain the single pages describing those jobs in which you are interested. They are available from your nearest Work Information Centre (the local CES can tell you where it is) or from the Careers Reference Centre in Flinders Lane near the City Square.

4   Read the job descriptions carefully and short-list those that appeal to you.

5   Find people who can tell you about the jobs you have selected.

6   Visit places where the jobs are carried out.

7   Seek work experience in the occupations you have chosen.

8   Note the formal training required. Is tertiary study needed? If so, what is the prerequisite educational standard for such a course? Are apprenticeships available? If so, what courses have to be taken in conjunction with them and where?

9   Visit the training institutions – many have special open days – and see if you would like to spend three or four years there.

10 Obtain course outlines and handbooks to read about specific units of study.

11 Be realistic about post-training opportunities. Who will employ you? Will you need to leave home? Is there a prospect of immediate employment or will you face stiff competition for relatively few positions?

Now, let us look at a case study.

Daisy was a forward-looking 14-year-old, individualistic and organised. The promotion of Victoria as 'The Garden State' led to her interest in the environment, but she did not want to be a gardener.

Careers in horticulture. Illustrator: Glenda Romeril.

She read the job descriptions in the CES *Job Guide* and listed the following as possible careers: agricultural secretary, botanist, florist, forester, flower grower, horticultural extension worker.

Floristry appealed to her artistic instincts and would involve working with people. There were no minimum educational standards to become an apprentice florist but she would have to find an employer willing to accept her. Her employment would be probationary for three months, after which apprenticeship indentures would be signed and registered. For part-time instruction, apprentice florists go to the White Horse College of TAFE in Box Hill for three years.

It is also possible to do full- or part-time courses in floristry at the Burnley campus of the Victorian College of Agriculture and Horticulture and the Melbourne School of Floristry but such courses do not guarantee employment, even if a Certificate of Proficiency is obtained.

Daisy also found out about the course for agricultural secretaries at the Glenormiston campus of VCAH. It is organised in conjunction with the Warrnambool College of TAFE and involves two years of full-time study to gain a Certificate of Business Studies (Agricultural Secretary). Entry requirements are successful completion of Year 11.

The remaining preferences which she had listed required Higher School Certificate with science subjects, so in Year 11, she kept her Mathematics options open and took Chemistry and Physics but kept up Art because she liked it. During the year she visited the university campuses (Melbourne, Monash, La Trobe and Deakin), the VCAH campuses (Burnley, Dookie, Glenormiston and Longerenong) and also the Rusden campus of Victoria College where a specialised Bachelor of Education degree in Environmental Studies can be taken. However, the place she really liked was the School of Forestry at Creswick.

Her parents were delighted that she was doing HSC although they were doubtful about the employment prospects for a girl in forestry. Daisy reminded them of equal opportunity legislation and argued that if she had a Botany major she could always teach secondary school science. No further objections.

One September, Daisy and her godmother were looking at the Spring Walk brochure distributed by the Botanic Gardens when godmother suddenly exclaimed: 'Anita Podwyszynski, a difficult name to pronounce!'

'Who is she?'

'A botanical artist.'

Daisy was interested.

'Are there many?'

Dozens! Margaret Stones, Joan Law-Smith, Jenny Phillips for a start. Next week a charming booklet, 'Artists from the Royal Botanic Gardens, Kew', arrived for Daisy and *The Man Who Painted Roses*, by Antonia Ridge, was set aside for her birthday.

Daisy thought about botanical art as a career. Then she realised that if there were botanical artists, there must also be botanical writers – for advertising copy, for magazine editors and even for books on gardens. (Later she discovered Vita Sackville-West, Mea Allen and Anne Scott-James.) On radio she heard Rosemary Davies, Kevin Heinze and Alan Gardiner. There was another possibility, horticultural extension work.

Well, what did she do? HSC results came out and her score was not high enough for Forestry so she took a Bachelor of Science degree with a Botany major. Then she worked as a botanist at Kings Park, Perth, for five years and she is now an extension officer with the Garden Advisory Service in the Department of Agriculture in Melbourne. She is also writing and illustrating a book on wildflowers.

And one other thing, she has changed her name to Marguerite.

NEXT WEEK: Another case study and a number of places where qualifications can be obtained.

The Age, 4 January 1985, Weekender, p. 5.

Looking at becoming a career horticulturalist

In the second of two articles about choosing a career, ALISON DALRYMPLE looks at a case study and lists places where qualifications can be obtained.

A career in horticulture provides opportunity to become involved in environmental quality and planning. Careers range from ornamental and amenity horticulture through landscape and park planning to economic crop production and marketing of nursery stock, fruit and vegetables, seeds and flowers.

When selecting a horticultural training course, a student should consider which of the following styles of career he or she prefers:

- A professional or executive career which will be the most challenging but which will involve substantially more office or laboratory work than field work.
- A supervisory or technical role under the direction of others and involving more work in the field.
- A trade position where all activity will be in the field and a lesser degree of responsibility is assumed.

Obviously the first category of job requires most formal study (usually a university degree); for the second, a diploma would be expected and for the third, a certificate. It is possible to move from the last-mentioned category to the others but a higher level of general education is needed.

A case study will illustrate this. Jonathan hated the school his parents had chosen for him. In fact, he hated his parents. They wanted him to be a doctor like his father and grandfather.

The rows got worse and Jonathan walked out. At 15 a drop-out? Not really. He simply wanted independence, the opportunity to be himself – but he needed a job, one without formal qualifications or experience. He was physically fit, he loved sport and he was observant.

Jonathan noticed the branches of a magnificent camphor laurel tree in his street being thinned. He reckoned the workmen were about his age and the job looked interesting with all the ropes, slings and chain saws. A sign said the tree was undergoing surgery.

He nipped back to the careers room at school and checked the CES *Job Guide* on being a tree surgeon. It read:

A tree surgeon is dedicated to the preservation of trees. His work involves pruning, removing, transplanting, feeding, fertilizing, cable-bracing and diagnosing tree problems. Personal requirements: fitness is important. A tree surgeon must have an interest in trees, a desire for outdoor work, a liking for heights, common sense when handling machinery, some intuition towards safety and climbing, desire for further knowledge and speed in thought and action.

Jonathan felt he matched this description and he got a casual job (mostly collecting the lopped branches) with a tree surgeon. His workmates had learnt on the job but they advised him to try for a horticultural apprenticeship and then do a further course in tree surgery.

He could go to either Collingwood College of TAFE or Oakleigh Technical School to gain a trade certificate in gardening or turf management, or nursery work or landscape gardening. The apprenticeship in turf management would train him to look after turf on golf courses, bowling greens, tennis courts and football and cricket grounds. He would learn about soils, drainage, grasses and fertilisers as well as the various mechanical devices (mowers, rollers, edgers, and watering systems). With his interest in sport, turf management sounded appealing.

Yet Jonathan was really more interested in trees and he was still arguing with his parents so he wanted to get away from Melbourne. He found that the Sunraysia College of TAFE offered a trade certificate in fruit growing. Once he had convinced a fruit grower to employ him Jonathan completed the four-year course while working and then he wanted to go further.

He investigated diploma courses, particularly the Diploma of Applied Science (Horticulture) at the Dookie campus of the Victorian College of Agriculture and Horticulture. This was a three-year full-time course with some specialisation in arboriculture or viticulture if he wished. However, entry required the Higher School Certificate which Jonathan decided to take on a part-time basis at night school. He studied General Mathematics, Chemistry, Physics, Biology and English.

With his practical experience and a good HSC pass, he was offered a place in the Bachelor of Forest Science course at Melbourne University where he spent his first year. The next two years he studied at the School of Forestry in Creswick and the final year was taken back in Melbourne.

Confident and with excellent qualifications, Jonathan wanted to travel. He spent some time as a ranger in Kakadu National Park in the Northern Territory and then he went to train foresters in Tamon Negara in Malaysia.

Now he is planning a trip to see the forests of the Soviet Union, Japan and the Americas and he wants to complete the National Diploma of Arboriculture given by the Royal Forestry Society in England.

Not bad for a school drop-out.

Extract from a letter

To Tommy Garnett, editor of the Gardening section of *The Age,* **14 December 1984:**

The fictitious cases became vivid personalities in their own right and romped away into novellas. I pruned them ruthlessly... All this self-indulgence had to be off-set by sober fact and earnest advice.

Apprenticeship courses

Oakleigh Technical School, corner North and Poath roads, Oakleigh.

Collingwood College of TAFE (Technical and Further Education). (Horticulture school, Oak Street, Royal Park). Trade Certificates in Gardening, Turf Management, Nurseryman or Nurserywoman, Landscape Gardening.

Whitehorse College of TAFE, 1000 White Horse Road, Box Hill. Trade Certificate in Floristry.

Sunraysia College of TAFE.
Advanced Trade Certificates in Citrus Growing, Viticulture, Greenkeeping, Landscape Construction, Propagation, Tree Surgery, Landscape Design.

Certificate courses

VCAH Glenormiston Campus.
Certificate of Business Studies (Agricultural Secretary).

Diploma courses

VCAH Dookie Campus.
Diploma of Applied Science in Food Production Horticulture.

VCAH Longerenong Campus.
Diploma of Applied Science in Agriculture.

VCAH Burnley Campus.
Diploma of Applied Science in Landscape Design, Diploma of Applied Science in Nursery Production and Management, Diploma of Applied Science in Park and Recreation Management.

Degree courses

Victoria College: Rusden campus.
Bachelor of Education (Environmental Studies).

Melbourne University.
Bachelor of Agricultural Science, Bachelor of Forest Science,

Bachelor of Science (Botany major), Master of Environmental Science.

La Trobe University.

Bachelor of Agricultural Science, Bachelor of Science (Botany major).

Monash University.

Bachelor of Arts (Botany major). Master of Environmental Science.

Deakin University.

Master of Science in Environmental Studies, Doctor of Philosophy in Environmental Studies.

Horticultural careers

A Superintendent of Parks and Gardens is responsible for plant production for the Melbourne City Council, for maintenance of plants within the central business district, for maintenance of parks, reserves, and plantations, and for the administration of plant nurseries.

A Horticultural Research Worker carries out research into the improvement of plant varieties, tree planting densities, tree shape and fertilisers; laboratory experiments, field trials and reading the appropriate literature are also part of the job.

A Retail Nurseryman is concerned with breeding, watering, cleaning and maintaining the appearance of the nursery, the stocking of shelves, setting up displays, propagating plants and satisfying customer needs in counter service and dispatching orders by road or rail.

A Horticultural Extension Worker is involved in writing regular gardening articles or

---

Extract from a letter

Received from principal of Oakleigh Technical School, 30 January 1985:

... I would like to thank you for your two excellent articles on horticulture that recently appeared in the Weekender ... Articles such as yours, so well researched and precise, are very helpful in assisting us promote these recently introduced courses.

news bulletins, preparing regular radio broadcasts, lecturing to garden clubs, attending field days and designing information leaflets on a variety of topics as well as answering letter and phone queries.

A Nurseryman establishes new plants from seed or cutting and progressively transfers the growing plant from trays in glasshouses to pots under glass frames and then to larger pots. He prepares soils and potting mixtures for planting seedlings and pot plants.

A Golf Course Curator cares for turf trees, fairways and greens and also for trees, shrubs and seedlings that enhance the grounds. He maintains the indoor plants for the clubhouse and the machinery that is used to care for the course.

The Age, 11 January 1985, Weekender, p. 7.

The art of nature printing

It is a pleasure to find a new reason for visiting Coolart, that delightful garden and bird sanctuary at Somers. Until 22 December [1985] the craft (or art) of nature printing is featured in *Pressed On Paper*, an exhibition highlighting the knowledge and expertise of the Museum of Victoria's current science and humanities scholar, Dr Eric Hochberg, who is curator of invertebrate zoology at the Santa Barbara Museum of Natural History in California.

In nature printing, images of natural objects are transferred to paper or cloth by inking the subject and then pressing paper on to it. The most favored themes are plants, insects and fish, although crustaceans, feathers and shells are also used.

The art of plant printing is more than 500 years old. Conrad von Butzbach's travel diary contains plant prints and Leonardo da Vinci used the technique to illustrate his *Codex Atlanticus*, published in 1510. Colonial America also fostered plant printing. Shrewd Benjamin Franklin printed plant leaves on paper money to prevent counterfeiting during the revolutionary period.

The exhibition at Coolart shows the best work of contemporary nature printers from the United States, Canada and Japan. The work of Robert Little is well represented with *Early Spring* (1970), a print of a bunch of seeds from *Ulmus fulva* found by the railroad track at Indian Head in Pennsylvania, and *Tropical Seed Pods*, printed in 1980 at Cutler Ridge in Florida. His *Geraniums* and *Datura candida* (done in Hawaii) use more than one color to good effect. Also memorable are Kay Langdon's *Wild Strawberries*, Evelyn Penington's *Rush and Wasp*, Louis Frey's *Poinciana* and Hochberg's delicate *Goat's Beard*.

Leaf printing was done in Australia last century. James Sinclair,

Nature print of *Aspidium hispidum*. Reproduced with permission from the archives of the Royal Botanic Gardens, Melbourne.

who worked on the Fitzroy Gardens, and his wife made a series of fern and eucalypt leaf prints in the 1860s and an amateur paleobotanist, Henry Deane, used leaf prints to illustrate his research.

I found the exhibition a happy conjunction of science and art. Supported by an information sheet and practical demonstration sessions, the exhibition will tour other parts of Australia next year.

The folio of Australian plants and fishes which Dr Hochberg is preparing will be eagerly sought by those who have fallen under the spell of this art.

Nature printing is a wonderful way to involve children in practical nature activities as it encourages scientific observation and artistic expression, and Coolart is a fine picnic place for the family.

The Age, 10 December 1985, Melbourne Living, p. 7.

Endangered species list grows

'You're joking?' My visitor was unbelieving. Six months ago I, too, would have scoffed at the suggestion that a plant in my garden, a honey-myrtle (*Melaleuca steedmanii*) could be under threat of extinction.

But for the work of the World Wildlife Fund (WWF), my ignorance would have continued. To me WWF meant pandas, not plants!

In 1984, however, the WWF launched an international program for plant conservation recognising that individual plants feed our world, cure our ills, provide materials for industry and generally enrich our lives.

The 24 WWF affiliates began to publicise the importance of plants and conserving them. In Spain, the focus was saving the flora of the Sierra Nevada mountains and rescuing the Granada Botanic Gardens; in South Africa, the purchase of a chain of reserves in Cape Province would protect endangered flora and in Sweden, new ways of saving the plants of the hay meadows were to be developed.

In Australia, the WWF financed the publication of *Extinct and Endangered Plants of Australia* by J. Leigh, R. Boden and J. Briggs. It also sponsored the brochure 'Rare and Endangered Plants in the Royal Botanic Gardens Melbourne' which was where I found *Melaleuca steedmanii* designated as endangered.

For effective work on the international level, WWF combines with the International Union for Conservation of Nature and Natural Resources (IUCN) and the United Nations Environment Program (UNEP). Together they published *The World Conservation Strategy of 1980*. There, guidelines for maintaining the delicate balance between conservation and development were defined.

Next, the *IUCN Plant Red Data Book* established the following plant classifications:

1   *Extinct*: where examples are not found after repeated searches in known and likely habitats.
2   *Endangered*: where a species appears in imminent danger of extinction.
3   *Vulnerable*: where preventative measures are necessary to save a species from the 'endangered' classification.
4   *Rare*: where the species forms small but stable populations not at present endangered or vulnerable but considered to be at risk.

This categorisation only applies to plants in natural habitats so my honey-myrtle is not, technically, endangered whereas its relations in Western Australia are facing extinction as the wheat belt extends in that state.

Of considerable interest in the Melbourne Botanic Gardens is *Sophora toromiro*. This species was thought to be extinct in its native Easter Island, but as the Melbourne specimen is producing seeds it is possible that the plant can be re-established in its island habitat once more.

The listings hold some surprises. The Monterey Cypress

Illustrator:
Glenda Romeril

(*Cupressus macrocarpa*) is on the rare list while Norfolk Island Pine (*Araucaria heterophylla*) and the Dragon's Tree (*Dracaena draco*) are on the vulnerable list.

In Australia, 78 species have become extinct since European settlement and another 201 species are likely to disappear through grazing, cropping, deforestation and mining activities.

The Threatened Plants Committee, based at the Royal Botanic Gardens in Kew, England, collates lists of rare and endangered plants now in cultivation in the major international botanic gardens, so encouraging the maintenance and exchange of genetic material. Australian botanic gardens are making their contribution to this work.

The estimate that 10 per cent of the world's flowering plants are threatened with extinction underlines the urgency of the conservation research and the need for widespread support.

The irony is that plant conservation projects are most needed in tropical countries but this is where they are least practised.

Against vegetation on such a lavish scale one small honey-myrtle seems inconsequential, but if I move house a large label will be left on it –

Endangered Species
No Pandas Without Plants

The Age, 11 February 1986, p. 30.

A resourceful way to learn about trees

I love Eucalyptus ficifolia, Eucalyptus melliodora,
Intertexta, radiata, todtiana and aggregata.
Have you seen them?
Can you say them?
Come on let's try more!

Environmental education already has a place in many Victorian classrooms. It is a subject that calls for participation by the wider community, and for this reason parents and youth leaders as well as teachers will welcome 'Trees and Forests', a recently released resource kit for schools, for the informative and imaginative material it offers 10- to 14-year-olds.

The kit has been produced as a joint venture by the Education Department and the Conservation, Forests and Lands Department with assistance from the Timber Promotions Council, the Pulp and Paper Manufacturers' Federation and the Victorian Sawmillers' Association.

Suggestions for more than 90 activities, reference material, case studies, an audio-cassette and a teachers' handbook are boxed in a bright green case. Supporting video material is also available separately.

Everywhere humor is well-judged for the age group. Puns that make an adult wince are a roaring success with 11-year-olds. 'Close Encounters of the Furred Kind', 'Raiders of the Lost Bark', and 'Meals in Wheels' are headings for just a few of the activities designed to heighten sensitivity to plants and wildlife.

Among the 'Games to Play', my young friends Meredith and Mark enjoyed Forest Car Rally which familiarised them with their own state both ecologically and geographically. 'You Are a Field Officer' introduced a career as well as giving practice in decision-making.

Immensely popular with Meredith and Mark were the tongue twisters ('Blue box, black butt, river red gum'), the tree slogans ('Learn not to burn'), and the tree jokes ('A sawmiller had his eye on a log – and a forester sat on it').

The handbook 'Forest for the Future' provides sound reference material and more complex activities which challenge the older students. Aspects of a lifestyle too often taken for granted are put up for consideration – the use of paper tissues or the choice of plastic toys in preference to wooden ones.

Dialogues on the audio-cassette point up the effect of our urban way of life on our natural resources, particularly forests. The touchy subject of protest is not evaded, and the future of the Errinundra forests is presented as a case study using extracts from media reports.

When launching the kit last month, Conservation, Forests and Lands Minister, Joan Kirner, said that the materials offered a complete and objective presentation of the issues without promoting any specific viewpoint.

Although I was critical of the amateurish standard of production on the audiotape, Meredith and Mark listened attentively and with obvious enjoyment.

At $35 the 'Trees and Forests' kit may seem expensive, but paper is expensive. That is why I hope one of the component student booklets, 'Forests and Forestry', might be sold separately to make up class sets. These can be re-used each year rather than photocopying reams of handouts for successive classes.

As something for a family to share, or for a school library, the total package is good value.

A close encounter of the furred kind. Illustrator: Glenda Romeril.

The Age, 14 October 1986, p. 34.

Indulge with simplicity

L et us indulge in all the glory of spring: in our gardens and, for those without gardens, in the spring harvest of cut flowers. This is the season to try flower arranging. Spring flower arrangements call for simplicity in form and effect, and in the choice of container.

The informal style is most appropriate – flowers aplenty, massed and set in a pool of light.

My choice for a spring container is sparkling glass with crystal clear water. If you are a traditionalist who simply must use stabilising aids for your arrangement, hide the container in a basket to create a freshly gathered effect.

In your mind, check out the key elements of your arrangement – shape, color, texture and appropriateness. The impact of your work results from the skilful integration of these elements.

For a spring arrangement, I favor a 'bouquet' shape as it gives a generous and extravagant impression reflecting the bounty of the season. As individual flowers need not be highlighted, interest comes from carefully considered color and from textural effects.

Everyone has an individual preference for colors, but flower arrangements are not seen in isolation. It is advisable to begin either with the color of the flowers and then decide their place in the room, or to select the setting for the flowers and then choose colors which complement it.

Room finishes, curtains, ornaments, even wood used in furniture may influence the color of the flowers you choose. Remember, too, the psychological effect of 'warm' and cool colors. Generally it is wise to keep to one group or the other.

Add interest and contrast by counterpointing textures – matt surfaces against glossy surfaces, fragile, translucent petals on the edge of the arrangement, more solid flowers in the middle. Include buds in a spring bowl, too, as they suggest the new life that spring brings.

If you are dependent on a florist for your cut flowers, choose your florist with care and cultivate his/her friendship. Note the general appearance of the shop and the quantity of the stock – fewer flowers may mean fresher flowers. Are the blooms carefully displayed so that you can assess their freshness by noting the crispness of uncluttered leaves? Look at the stamens and avoid dark ones laden with pollen.

Flowers should be the last item on your shopping list, to minimise the time they will be out of water. The way a florist wraps the flowers you choose is another test of professional knowledge. If the florist is reliable then the preparation of the flowers for your arrangement will be minimal, but it is advisable to re-cut the stem to remove any air bubble or seal that may prevent the flower taking up water.

Some flowers require special conditioning treatment and here again a good florist will be able to help you if you inquire. Bulb flowers can be a bit temperamental, so cut the stem back to the green part and wash away the slimy sap under

was trampled (thereafter her sovereign dubbed her 'the All Powerful').

There was also Alexandrine, who grew 67 varieties of sweet pea at Boulogne; Julie, who designed much of the wonderful garden at Pregny; Miriam, whose Ashton Wold is an exemplary present-day wildflower garden; and Beth, who is restoring Waddesdon. And that's only the women!

All the Rothschilds were devotees of heated glasshouses and the propagation of exotic plants. Among them were botanists, horticulturists and natural historians. Miriam's great-uncle Leopold specialised in waterlilies at Gunnersbury; her uncle Walter introduced kangaroos, emus and cassowaries into the park at Tring; her father Charles collected irises and orchids; his cousin Lionel made Exbury synonymous with rhododendrons.

But two wars and the Nazi regime brought disruption, privation, dislocation and loss. Of the main European gardens, only Villa Ile de France is intact. The rest were given away or sold. In England, many of the finest were sold or went to the National Trust.

Permeating the book are the memories of a sensitive child, a

Waddesdon Manor, England – a Rothschild garden. Photographer: Helen Botham.

feeling young woman and a notable naturalist. The wit, humor and humanity of a lifetime enliven the pages. The past is celebrated with no regret.

The writing has a staccato, restless intensity rather than a seamless literary style, but its sense of family and unstudied enthusiasm give this book its own measure of Rothschild *panache*.

Nina Crone

The Age, 5 April 1997, Extra, p. 12.